Martin Luther
HERO OF FAITH

W9-BRX-347

MARTIN LUTHER
Hero of Faith

Written by
FREDERICK NOHL

Illustrated by
RICHARD HOOK

SAINT LOUIS

Concordia Publishing House, St. Louis, Missouri

Copyright 1962 by Concordia Publishing House

Library of Congress Catalog Card No. 62-14146

7 8 9   97

Manufactured in the United States of America

TO H. H. G.,
himself a hero of faith

Contents

A Word About
Great Men

W E cannot look, however imperfectly, upon a great man without gaining something by him."

Thomas Carlyle, a Scottish essayist and historian, wrote these words over 100 years ago. They are as true today as they were then.

Take yourself, for example. You listen to a great man speak. Or you read about him. Or maybe you even talk with him. How this thrills you! And how often this leads you to promise yourself: "I'm going to try my best to be like him."

We all need heroes, great men and women whom we can look up to and in whose footsteps we can follow. These heroes of ours may be living — a parent, a teacher, an explorer, the mayor of our town, a famous army officer, a jet pilot, a navy nurse. Or they may be dead — dead, that is, except as they live on in our hearts and lives.

The best place to find heroes is in God's Book, the Bible. Here we find the perfect Hero, Jesus Christ, God's Son and the world's Savior. Here we also find heroes of faith who lived their lives for God, men and women like Abraham, David, Daniel, Mary the mother of Jesus, Lydia, and Paul.

But the Bible does not tell about all the great men and women of God. It does not mention all who lived in Bible times. And, of course, many, many Christians have lived and died since the Bible's last chapter was written.

One of these is Martin Luther. Born of humble parents in little Eisleben, Germany, on November 10, 1483, Martin Luther grew up to live the adventuresome, often dangerous life of a man of God. He became a man whose life taught many a lesson to others. He became, in other words, one of those great men whom to know is to gain something unusually worthwhile.

Martin Luther still lives on today. He lives on most strongly in the lives of Christians who carry his name — the Lutherans. But he also lives on in the lives of many others throughout the world, for his thoughts and words and actions have helped to make our modern world what it is.

This is the great man, the hero of faith, whose story I am going to tell in the pages that follow. As you look at Martin Luther, remember that you will not be looking at a god, but at a man of God. Not at a perfect man, but at an imperfect man, one who knew his own weaknesses and sins only too well. Not at a man who depended on himself, but at one who believed that through Christ he could do all things.

And as you look, may you also learn.

FREDERICK NOHL

Martin Luther
HERO OF FAITH

1. Martin Comes and Grows

T HE baby's first cries echoed from wall to wall, warming the whole house on that cold November day in 1483. Hans Luther, copper miner in little Eisleben, Germany, smiled nervously at his wife Margaret. Her tired eyes returned his smile, even as they mirrored her prayer of thanks for having safely given birth to a second child — a son, no less.

On the very next day, Hans carefully bundled his newborn boy in the warmest blankets he could find. Closing the door of his house behind him, he quickly walked the two windy blocks to St. Peter's Church. Here, on November 11, the festival of St. Martin of Tours, the proud father handed his son to the priest. "Martin Luther," chanted the priest as he three times poured water on the child's wrinkled forehead, "I baptize thee in the name of the Father, and of the Son, and of the Holy Ghost."

The baptism over, Hans headed for home, snugly cradling little Martin in his brawny arms. Urged on by the biting wind, Hans arrived home in short order. Walking to his wife's bedside, he gently handed her the whimpering baby. "Here,

Margaret, take our Martin and care for him. And pray that no evil will come to him. For who knows what plans God has for him?"

Hans, Margaret, and Martin

Hans Luther had not always been a miner. He had been born into a peasant family, working the family farmlands with his father and three younger brothers. Since the estate always went to the youngest son, Hans had no chance of inheriting any of his father's property. Therefore, after marrying Margaret, Hans decided to move to Eisleben. Here he found work in the copper mines that tunneled their way under the hilly, wooded Thuringian countryside.

However, Hans did not stay in Eisleben. In the spring of 1484, when Martin was only six months old, Hans moved his family to Mansfeld, another copper-mining center about five miles northwest of Eisleben. In Mansfeld Hans hoped to make a better living. By working long and hard and by being thrifty, he improved his position slowly but surely.

Hans's neighbors respected him. They even elected him to serve on the Mansfeld city council. After 1500 Hans was able to rent and operate his own mines and smelting furnaces. He also bought his own house, thus providing a permanent home for his wife and, by this time, seven children.

Martin Luther's parents, like those of many other children in his day, were very religious. The family regularly attended Mass at St. George's Church, listening to the priest chant the Communion service in Latin. At home the parents prayed with and for Martin and their other children. Unfortunately neither Martin's home training nor his later school years helped him to find in Jesus a forgiving, loving Savior. Rather he thought of Jesus as a severe judge, kept from punishing Christians only by His mother Mary and by John the Baptist. This picture of Jesus often terrified Martin, as did the stories of evil spirits and witches that supposedly roamed the countryside.

4

Martin, again like most other children of his day, was expected to obey his parents without question. When he failed to do so, they whipped him severely. Once Martin stole a nut. His mother became so angry that she beat him till the blood came. Another time Martin even ran away from home for a few days after his father had punished him. In spite of such unpleasant moments, Martin's home life was often a happy one, filled with singing and laughter. Hans and Margaret Luther loved their children and raised them as best they knew how.

Elementary School Days

When Martin was four and a half, his parents enrolled him in the Mansfeld Latin school. This was an unusually early age, for most boys did not begin school until they were six or seven. Nicolaus Oemler, a young friend of the Luther family, often carried little Martin the few blocks to school.

Although Martin spoke German at home and among his friends, he learned and used Latin in the Mansfeld school. His teacher gave him a Latin primer and taught him simple prayers and hymns. By the time Martin had finished sixth grade, he knew most of the Mass well and could speak and write Latin with ease. Further study increased his understanding of religious music, ancient literature, history, and those parts of the Bible that were used in the church services. When Martin finished his last class at the Mansfeld school, he had been trained to be a faithful church member.

While at school, Martin and his fellow pupils had to work hard and to obey their teacher's every order. Sometimes the teacher would hang a little wooden donkey around the neck of the pupil whose work was the poorest. During his early school years, Martin had to make a mark on a slate each time he did not know his lesson or failed to follow his teacher's wishes. At the end of the week his slate would be "wiped clean," but only after the teacher had spanked him, once for

5

each mark. At one time, Luther's record showed fifteen marks. He remembered that weekend well into his later years.

When Martin moved to the middle and higher grades, the number of spankings decreased. Instead, he and other pupils had to pay fines if they misbehaved. Since few of the pupils had money of their own, this meant asking their parents to pay the fines. Many, therefore, got their spankings at home.

A Year in Magdeburg

By the time Martin was fourteen, his father Hans had become a respected and fairly well-to-do citizen of Mansfeld. Hans Luther took a real interest in his children's education, including Martin's. Because he had heard that the schools in Saxony were very good, and because he wanted his son to attend several different schools, Hans sent Martin to Magdeburg, sixty miles from home.

Martin and his friend John Reinecke traveled the road from Mansfeld to Magdeburg on foot. Magdeburg was one of the larger cities of Germany, with about twelve thousand inhabitants. It had so many churches and chapels and celebrated so many religious festivals that some called it "Little Rome," thus comparing it to the center of the Western Christian Church.

In Magdeburg, Martin and John attended the Cathedral School. Several of the teachers at this school belonged to the Brethren of the Common Life. The Brethren were mystics who believed in much Bible reading and in living simple, holy lives. While studying here, Martin saw his first complete Bible. Because Bibles were so expensive, they were usually found only in libraries or in the homes of priests and wealthy people. Often the Bibles were chained to library tables so that they could not be misplaced or stolen.

Although Martin's parents could well afford to support him, he regularly joined other boys in begging for food. People were used to having students ask for help, and were not surprised to hear a group singing for their supper. One Christmas day, Martin and some of his friends went from house to house singing carols. They stopped in front of a farmer's hut. The farmer, after listening to the songs, came out with some food. He couldn't find the boys right away, and so he shouted, "Boys, where are you?" Thinking the farmer was angry with them for disturbing him, Martin and his friends started to run away. But the man continued calling. Soon the boys realized that he was not angry, and so they came back to claim their gifts.

St. George's School in Eisenach

Martin left Magdeburg at the end of one year. For some unknown reason Hans Luther had his son transfer to a school in Eisenach.

Eisenach was a walled city in Thuringia, located southwest of Mansfeld. A castle known as the Wartburg looked down on this town of over two thousand people. Once much used, the Wartburg was now falling into ruin. In spite of its condition, however, it was destined to become a place of safety for Martin Luther.

Martin enrolled in the Latin school of St. George's Church. Here he prepared himself well for the university work to come. One of his favorite teachers was John Trebonius, the rector, or principal. Men like Trebonius helped make Martin's three-year stay at Eisenach one of the happiest periods of his life, one he often talked about in later years.

Once Martin delivered a speech in Latin, welcoming Professor Jodocus Trutvetter of the University of Erfurt to St. George's School. He did so well that the honored visitor urged Trebonius: "Keep an eye on that Luther. There is something in that boy. By all means prepare him for the university and send him to us at Erfurt."

Trutvetter then turned to Martin and said: "My son, the Lord has bestowed special gifts on you; use them faithfully in His service. When you are ready and wish to come to us at

7

Erfurt, remember that you have a good friend there, Doctor Jodocus Trutvetter. Appeal to him, he will give you a friendly reception."

As he had done in Magdeburg, Martin occasionally joined other students in street singing and begging for food. Among those who heard and liked his singing was Ursula Cotta, the wife of a prosperous businessman. Mrs. Cotta was related to the Schalbe family, whose little son, Henry, Martin regularly tutored. In this way the young Luther became a close friend of both the Cottas and the Schalbes. In fact, he lived in the Cotta home and ate his meals with the Schalbes. Such friendly surroundings added many pleasant moments to Martin's life in Eisenach.

The University Years

Martin Luther graduated from high school in the spring of 1501. Eager to continue his schooling, he was happy when his father allowed him to attend the University of Erfurt. Not only did many consider Erfurt to be the best university in all Germany, but it was also close to Mansfeld, the family home. Moreover, Martin knew that he had a good friend at Erfurt, Doctor Jodocus Trutvetter.

Martin joined nearly two thousand other students when he enrolled at the university in May 1501. In September 1502, when Martin was not quite nineteen years old, the university awarded him the Bachelor of Arts degree. There were fifty-seven students in his class, and at the time of graduation, Martin ranked thirtieth. Further years of hard study led to the Master of Arts degree early in 1505. This time there were seventeen graduates, and among them Martin ranked second.

His general education finished, Martin now had to decide whether to teach or to continue his studies. Hans Luther was pleased with the progress his son had made. He wanted Martin to continue studying to become a lawyer. This would cost additional money, but Hans was ready to spend it. Since Martin had already studied a little law, and because he wanted to respect his parents' wishes, he agreed to continue his work at Erfurt.

But the Lord had other plans for Martin Luther. The hard-working student soon discovered that he did not really care to study law. Often he found himself reading books on other subjects.

Then one day the young law student sold all his books. Next he called together his friends for a special banquet. The following day Martin Luther left the university. Soon after, his parents received a message that not only troubled them but also angered them.

What had happened?

2. St. Anne's Monk

O<small>N</small> July 17, 1505, Martin Luther and a few close friends left the University of Erfurt grounds. Perhaps some traveler noticed the companions arguing with Luther. As the traveler passed the group, he might have caught these words: "Martin, you don't have to do this. . . . Think of what your father will say. . . . You'll make such an able lawyer. . . . Don't throw away your life. . . ."

But Luther's mind was made up. He had no intention to go back on his words of the day before: "Today you see me for the last time and then no more."

So Luther said little. Finally the men reached a well-known group of buildings — the monastery or cloister of St. Augustine in Erfurt. Now Luther turned to his friends, shook their hands, spoke a few words of farewell, and left them. With tear-filled eyes they watched him walk slowly through the open gates.

Luther had put behind him the world he could no longer face. He had gone through the gates to a world where he hoped to make peace with God. Martin Luther had decided to become a monk.

The Troubled Soul

Luther's decision to leave the study of law came suddenly. Yet this decision had its real beginnings early in his childhood. Luther's parents had taught him to fear the witches, elves, and spirits that supposedly caused storms and disease, tempted men to sin, and even stole food from the family supply. His church and its teachers had taught him to fear hell and purgatory and the God who cast men there.

True, the church had also taught Luther how to escape these terrors and to gain the joys of heaven. "God the Son has died for the sins of the world," her teachers had said. "This makes God the Father willing to pardon those who come to Him." But how was the repentant sinner to find the Father? He dared not approach the terrible Judge directly. Even Jesus was often so angry at sin that He would not carry a man's prayers to the Father. "Therefore," Luther's teachers had told him, "ask some of the saints already in heaven to go to Jesus with your prayer for the Father's forgiveness. And since the saint closest to Jesus is His own mother Mary, pray to her more than to any other.

"But remember, Martin, just to pray by yourself is not enough. The church has to pray for you too. Even when the priest has asked that you be forgiven, God will not listen unless you do good works. The more gifts you give to the church and to the poor, the more trips you make to Rome and Jerusalem, and the more pleasures you give up, the better will be your chances for heaven. The best and safest way to do all this, and the one that is most God pleasing, is to give up everything and become a monk."

Luther was not one to forget or treat lightly such matters. He took them seriously, too seriously. Often he had sleepless nights because he felt his sins were still not forgiven. If only he could be sure!

When Luther decided to become a monk, he was simply taking a step which he hoped would clear his conscience of all fear and doubt. It was also a step which certain events in his life had helped him take. For example, in the streets of Magdeburg he once saw a ragged, barefoot, dying prince begging, begging because he believed that this would help him earn forgiveness. Luther never forgot the scene. Later in life he said, "Whoever looked at him was deeply moved and felt ashamed of his worldly way of life."

Another time a close friend of Luther died suddenly. His

death troubled Luther deeply. "What if *I* should die?" he asked himself. "Would I be ready? Would I be able to stand before the terrible Judge?"

Then, too, there was that eventful hour early in July 1505. Luther had visited his home in Mansfeld. Now, on a warm and sultry day, he was on his way back to Erfurt. As he walked along, he saw the sky slowly fill with black, racing clouds. Before long he felt raindrops streaking his cheeks. And then a violent storm began. Lightning bolts and thunder filled the heavens with light and noise. Luther was terrified. In his mind he saw visions of raging devils, an angry God, and the terrors of hell prepared for the unforgiven sinner. He fell to the ground and cried: "St. Anne, mother of Mary, help me! I promise to become a monk."

"Are You, Martin Luther, Ready . . . ?"

As a monk Martin Luther would now make his home in a monastery. Monasteries (also called cloisters, chapters, or convents) were the homes of men and women who had left their families and friends to live a quiet, well-ordered, religious life. These people believed that this kind of life would bring them closer to God and preserve them from the sinful world.

The monastery that Luther entered belonged to the Augustinian Order of Hermits. This order, or grouping of monasteries, had been founded in Italy in 1287 and had been named after St. Augustine, a great monk and bishop. (A. D. 354—430)

For the first two months Luther was on trial. Other monks watched him closely, and he was given a chance to think over his decision. But by September 1505 Luther was ready to present himself as a novice, or beginner. The prior, or head of the monastery, stood on the steps of the monastery altar. In the presence of all the monks Luther stepped forward and fell to the floor at the prior's feet.

"What are you looking for?" the prior asked.

"God's grace and your mercy," Luther answered.

"Are you married?"

"No."

"Do you owe anybody any work or money?"

"No."

"Do you have any secret diseases?"

"No."

"The life you are about to take up will be a hard one. You will no longer be able to do as you please, your food will be skimpy, and you will have to wear rough clothes. During the day you will have to work hard, and at night you will have to spend long hours in prayer. You will have to fight sin, you can never marry, you will be poor and forced to beg, and you will be lonely. Are you, Martin Luther, ready to accept these hardships?"

"Yes, with God's help, and insofar as human weakness allows."

At these words the choir began to chant. A monk shaved a circle of hair from Luther's head, and another gave him a black skullcap to wear. Luther took off his regular clothes and replaced them with a monk's habit, a white robe under a black cloak, both held to the body by a leather belt. Then he knelt before the altar as the prior prayed for him.

When the choir sang the closing hymn, Luther fell flat on the floor, arms outstretched in the form of a cross. After the hymn, Luther's fellow monks welcomed him with a kiss of peace, and the prior spoke these final words of warning and encouragement: "Not he that has begun, but he that endures to the end shall be saved."

Luther, clothed in black, had become a monk in the Black Cloister in Erfurt.

Luther Becomes a Priest

Luther was a novice for the first year. During this time he learned all the monastery rules and customs. His little room, or cell, had only a table, chair, and bed. Here he spent many hours alone, praying, reading, meditating. He could speak only at certain times. Seven times a day Luther joined other monks for worship in the chapel. He helped clean and repair the cloister buildings and grounds. The days passed quietly and quickly. Luther's troubled soul grew more peaceful.

At the end of the year Luther became a full-fledged Augustinian monk. In another special ceremony he again promised to obey God and his superiors, never to marry, and to give up all personal property. Not long after Luther had taken his vows as a monk, the prior picked Luther to become a priest. To prepare himself properly for this work, Luther began long hours of private study. Finally, in May 1507 he was ready to celebrate his first Communion service, or Mass.

Among the worshipers was Hans Luther. Although Luther's father was not yet fully pleased with the life his son had chosen, he had come to Erfurt with twenty horsemen. He had also made a gift of $300 to the cloister.

The Mass began. Luther stepped before the altar. He recited the opening parts of the service without difficulty. But suddenly he came to the words, "We offer unto Thee, the living, the true, the eternal God." The idea that he, a sinner, would dare to approach the holy God was too much. Luther thought to himself: "How shall I address God, seeing that all men ought to tremble in the presence of even an earthly prince? Who am I, that I should lift up my eyes or raise my hands to God? The angels surround Him. At His nod the earth trembles. And shall I, a miserable little pygmy, say, 'I want this, I ask for that'? I am dust and ashes and full of sin, and I am to speak to the living, eternal, and true God." Luther was so terrified that he barely managed to finish the Mass.

Tired and still shaken, Luther joined his father and friends. During dinner he told his father, "My new life is so quiet and godly."

When Hans Luther heard this, his temper rose. "You learned scholar," he said, "have you never read in the Bible that you should honor your father and your mother? And here you have left me and your dear mother to look after ourselves in our old age."

Luther replied: "But, Father, I could do you more good by prayers than if I had stayed in the world. And don't forget that a voice from heaven called me to this life when I was in the storm."

Hans Luther was not convinced. He remarked, "God grant that it was not a trick of the devil."

Back to School

By this time Luther had been away from the University of Erfurt for two years. Now he returned there to continue his schooling. But he did not go back to study law. Rather he took courses that led to the Bachelor of Arts in the Bible degree. This degree would permit him to deliver elementary lectures on the Bible.

In the fall of 1508 John Staupitz asked Luther to teach philosophy at the University of Wittenberg, even though Luther had not yet finished his course at Erfurt. Staupitz, vicar-general, or leader, of the Augustinian order in Germany, was also dean of the university. He regularly visited the Erfurt cloister and had come to know Luther as a good student and faithful monk. Therefore when Wittenberg needed a temporary teacher, Staupitz believed that Luther could do the job.

Wittenberg, about sixty miles north and seventy miles east of Erfurt, was the main city of Saxony. It had gotten its name, which means "white mountain," because of a sandy hill nearby. Located on a sharp bend in the Elbe River, this walled city housed about 2,100 people. It was less than a mile long, or about a ten-minute walk. Frederick the Wise, the Elector of Saxony, considered Wittenberg his prize possession. When he became ruler, he began a building program to improve the city. There in 1502 he founded a university to be staffed by members of the Augustinian order.

17

When Luther arrived at the university, he found much of it uncompleted. Law classes met in the elector's castle. Students also went to classes in the partly finished Augustinian monastery. Only one regular building had been completed. Students and faculty worshiped at the Castle Church. This church was first built in 1343 to house a thorn supposedly from Jesus' crown. However, in 1490 Frederick decided to rebuild the church completely. The work was not finished until 1509 and cost about $2,500,000.

The Teacher and the Student

Besides teaching his classes, Luther continued his studies. The more he studied the writings of the early church fathers, the less they satisfied him. And the more he studied the Bible, the more he believed that it alone had the final answers to life's problems. Very likely during this first stay at Wittenberg Luther began to sense that God could be found only in the Bible, not in the teachings of men.

Luther also received some comforting advice during this period at Wittenberg. For some time after entering the monastery Luther's troubled conscience seemed at rest. But then he again began to wonder whether God was really pleased with him. He fasted for days, he spent sleepless nights in prayer, he beat himself — all to fight the sins that constantly tempted him. Once he locked himself in his room as punishment. A few days later his fellow monks forced the door open and found him — unconscious! Yet he could not feel that God loved him or that he was doing enough to be saved.

Even the thought of Christ continued to frighten Luther. As he himself later said: "The name of Christ often frightened me, and, when I looked on Him and the cross, He seemed to me like a flash of lightning. When people mentioned His name, I would rather have heard the devil mentioned. For I believed that I would have to do good works until they made Christ love and forgive me."

One day, when Luther felt especially low, an older priest spoke to him in words that Luther never forgot. "Martin," he said, "don't you remember the Apostles' Creed? Don't you know that it shows that God loved you enough to send His Son to save you? Haven't you often said, 'I believe in the forgiveness of sins'? Martin, don't torture yourself with your sins. Throw yourself into the Savior's arms — the Savior who died for you!"

In any case, as reward for his thorough study the University of Wittenberg faculty awarded Luther the Bachelor of Arts in the Bible degree in March 1509. Seven months later Luther went back to Erfurt. Here he taught at the university and at the same time continued his studies. He soon earned a second and even a third graduate degree.

Luther taught and studied at Erfurt for three semesters. And then one day he was told something that made him especially happy: "Luther, you are going to Rome!"

The Trip to Rome

To understand why Luther went to Rome, we must first know what was happening to the German Augustinian monasteries. Not all the monks lived the same way. Some monasteries were very strict. Others cared little about following the order's rules. In 1510 Egidio, the general of the whole Augustinian order, ordered all the German monasteries to agree to a new constitution, or set of rules. But some of the strict monasteries, including Luther's, refused to go along. They feared that the new constitution was too weak and that it would cause even the strict monasteries to become careless.

Luther and a fellow professor first went to Halle, not far from Eisleben, to complain to a church leader. But the strict monasteries were not satisfied with just a trip to Halle — they felt that they had to send representatives directly to the general in Rome. They chose two men, an older monk and Luther.

In November 1510 these two started out from Nuernberg for Holy Rome, the Eternal City.

About 850 miles of walking lay ahead of them. Many of the miles were through the windswept mountain passes of the snow-covered Alps. Although warm weather awaited them in Rome, its warmth could not help them as they fought the cold winds of late fall. Fortunately they did not often have to sleep outside. Many monasteries along the way offered travelers a chance to rest and refresh themselves. Southward they traveled for forty days — through Bavaria, across the Swiss mountains, through the Italian cities of Milan and Florence. Finally, at the turn of the year Luther got his first view of Rome. He threw himself to the ground and said, "Greetings to you, Holy Rome!"

Rome, over 2,000 years old, was a city of some 40,000 people. Once the mighty capital of the great Roman Empire, the city had lost much of its former glory. But Luther cared little about this. He was in Rome to feed and comfort his troubled soul, to carry back with him the blessings it offered to devout pilgrims. Here were seventy monasteries and dozens of churches with their countless relics offering escape from the terrors of purgatory. Here were the catacombs, the underground caves where thousands of early Christians were buried. Here lived the cardinals and, above all, the Holy Father, Pope Julius II. What more could a Christian want?

How disappointed Luther became as the days passed by! He and his companion presented their request to General Egidio the day after they arrived. Off and on for four weeks the general discussed the matter with them. But most of the time was their own, to do with much as they pleased. Luther visited church after church, saying masses in them whenever he could. On hands and knees he climbed the twenty-eight steps that Jesus was supposed to have used when taken before Pilate. He walked through the catacombs and visited the graveyards of the saints.

Luther saw — or thought he saw — many wonderful relics: a crucifix that had once spoken, the chain that had held St. Paul, the grave of the Samaritan woman whom Jesus met at the well, the rope used to drag Jesus to the cross, eleven thorns from Jesus' crown, a nail from His cross, blood and water from His side, and some hair of the Virgin Mary. He also saw the stone that had sealed Christ's grave, the rope Judas used to hang himself, a few twigs from the burning bush of Moses, and one of the thirty pieces of silver paid Judas for a kiss.

The more Luther saw and heard, the more uncomfortable he began to feel. Were the stories about the crimes of some of the popes and cardinals really true? Why did so many of the priests and monks say Masses so carelessly? Did the relics really release people from the pains of purgatory? Why did some of the priests smile when they saw that he believed in the power of Masses and relics? Why, after climbing the stairs of Pilate and saying an Our Father for his dead grandfather on each, did he think as he reached the last step, "Who knows whether this is true?" Why was he having all these doubts in Holy Rome? Luther still believed that the church was God's, but he began to wonder whether all the church taught and did was really pleasing to God.

After four weeks, General Egidio finally reached a decision about the German Augustinian monasteries. "No," he said, "the strict monasteries cannot remain separate. They must join with the others as I have ordered." Their request denied, the two men left Rome, arriving in Nuernberg at the end of March 1511. At Nuernberg Luther left his friend and continued on to Erfurt. Soon he was back to his teaching and his studies.

But he couldn't stop wondering about what he had seen and heard in Rome.

3. The Sound of a Hammer

AFTER returning from Rome, Martin Luther stayed in Erfurt only a few months. In the summer of 1511 John Staupitz ordered him back to Wittenberg.

Staupitz's order was a real turning point in Luther's life. From this time on Luther called Wittenberg his home. Before too many years, people would think of Luther when they heard the name Wittenberg, and of Wittenberg when they heard the name Luther.

Professor Martin Luther

Martin moved into the Augustinian monastery in Wittenberg. One day Staupitz met him under a pear tree in the monastery garden. "Luther," he said, "I want you to become a preacher and a regular professor at the university. Therefore you must study for the Doctor of Theology degree."

Staupitz's words frightened Luther. He tried to get out of the assignment. "Doctor Staupitz," he argued, "I'm not the man for this. I'm too young. My body isn't strong enough to do the work. What you're doing is taking my life; I won't be able to stand the strain for even three months."

Dr. Staupitz knew that Luther was frightened, but also that what Luther said was not really true. So with a smile he answered: "Martin, don't you know the Lord has many important things to do? And if He is to do them, He's going to need good advisers. So even if you should die, you can be His helper in heaven."

Luther continued to argue. But finally he gave in to his leader's wishes. He promised to practice his preaching and to continue his studies.

Martin had preached to the monks while at Erfurt, but always in private. Now he was to preach in public. He preached his trial sermon in the monastery dining room. The monks approved it. Soon Luther was appointed the official monastery preacher. From then on he delivered his sermons in an old wooden chapel on the monastery grounds.

Those who heard Luther's sermons soon noticed that they were different from those of many other preachers. News of his preaching spread beyond the monastry grounds. Before long the chapel was filled to overflowing. More and more people came to hear this powerful preacher, this man who told them more about the forgiveness of sins through Jesus Christ than they had ever heard before.

In 1514 Luther moved out of the rickety chapel and into St. Mary's Church, also called the Town Church. Here there was room for all who wanted to hear Luther. And by 1516 people were hearing him preach almost every day.

While Luther preached, he also continued studying. In fact, by October 1512 Luther had passed all the tests for the Doctor of Theology degree. After a colorful ceremony in the Castle Church, the University of Wittenberg awarded him the diploma for which he had worked five long years. As *Doctor* Martin Luther left the church, his fellow students grabbed him. They placed him on their shoulders and carried him through the streets, while the town bell added its note of congratulation.

A few days later Staupitz saw the last of his instructions to Luther fulfilled. On October 22 Luther began a lifetime of service as professor of the Bible at the University of Wittenberg — a lifetime that saw this university become the most talked about in all Europe.

The Light in the Tower

Luther had been busy before, but now he became busier than ever. As we have seen, he preached regularly. He also instructed and supervised the novices, or beginners, who joined the Wittenberg monastery. In 1515 he began to supervise eleven Augustinian monasteries. This meant much travel and letter writing. On top of all this he had to attend to his main job: preparing and delivering lectures on the Bible to the university students.

Busy though they were, these early years in Wittenberg were perhaps the most important in Luther's whole life. For now he dug deeply into the Bible. Already during his first term in Wittenberg, 1508 and 1509, Luther had come to believe that the Bible is more important than the teachings of the church fathers. This belief grew stronger as he studied Genesis, the Psalms, and Paul's letters to the Romans and the Galatians — and as he taught his students about these Bible books.

One day in 1514 Luther was studying the Letter to the Romans. As usual he was in his private office, a room on the second floor of a tower attached to the monastery. As he worked his way through the first chapter he came to verses sixteen and seventeen. Here he read: "I am not ashamed of the Gospel: It is the power of God for salvation to everyone who has faith,

25

to the Jew first and also to the Greek. For in it the righteousness of God is revealed through faith for faith, as it is written [Habakkuk 2:4], 'The righteous shall live by faith.'"

Luther paused. "Now wait a minute," he told himself. "What does Paul mean when he talks about the 'righteousness of God'? And how does man become righteous or just before God? Oh, I know. God shows His righteousness by punishing sinners every time they do wrong. And the only way a man can become righteous is to do all that God wants him to do.

"But no, that can't be right. Paul says that man is made righteous or just by faith, by believing in something that God has done for him. Well, what has God done for man to make him righteous or holy? Let me see now. Paul says that the Gospel is the power that saves. Now what does the Gospel talk about? Oh, yes, it tells me about Jesus Christ. Jesus kept the Law perfectly, and yet He was punished on the cross. But why? Because He had done something wrong? No, because I had.

"I see the answer! God punished Jesus in my place, the same Jesus who had kept God's holy Law. By punishing His Son, God has carried out His threat that sin will be punished by death. All I have to do is accept this fact, and I need not fear that God will punish me with eternal death. I am holy in God's sight because I know and believe that Jesus is holy for me and has taken my punishment."

Luther had just had his great "tower experience." He had finally found the answer to the question that had tortured him for so long: "How can I be sure that God has forgiven my sin and that He loves me?" Now at last he could escape from the fears that had driven him into the monastery almost ten years before.

The light Luther had found in the tower grew from a flickering spark to a roaring fire as the years passed by. The first object it burned was a man named Tetzel. But to understand why and how, we must first look at certain events that were taking place in Europe.

Albert, Archbishop of Mainz

About a year before Luther's "tower experience" three important German church officers died. They were the bishop of Halberstadt and the archbishops of Magdeburg and Mainz.

One of the German electors, Joachim of Brandenburg, set out to win these positions. He planned to have his brother Albert appointed to all three by Pope Leo X. However, church laws did not allow any person to hold more than one office at a time. Also, Albert was only 23, below the age that archbishops were supposed to be. Nevertheless, Joachim believed that if he offered the pope enough money, Albert would get the three appointments.

How right Joachim was! By December 1513 Albert was bishop of Halberstadt and archbishop of Magdeburg at a cost of about $25,000. But to become archbishop of Mainz took longer and cost much more money. Others also wanted the position, the highest in all Germany. Not only did the archbishop of Mainz head the German church, he was one of seven German electors who together elected the emperor.

To become archbishop of Mainz usually meant that one had to contribute $300,000 to the church at Rome. Albert therefore said, "I'm willing to pay this, and I'll add another $250,000 besides."

When Pope Leo heard this, he quickly made up his mind. "Albert," the pope decided, "is the only man for the job." And so Albert of Brandenburg became the new archbishop of Mainz.

Actually neither Albert nor his brother had $550,000 to contribute. But they were able to borrow what they needed from the Fuggers, a family of German bankers. To help them pay back the money, Leo allowed Albert to give out indulgences in much of Germany for eight years. Any money received from the indulgences was to be divided: one half was to go to the Fuggers as payment on Albert's huge debt; the other half was to go to the pope, to be used for the building of St. Peter's Church in Rome.

27

Thus Joachim and Albert got what they wanted — control of the German church and a second electoral vote. Pope Leo also got what he wanted — money to spend for himself and for St. Peter's Church. And the people of Germany got what they didn't need but thought they wanted — indulgences.

Indulgences

Indulgences were part of a church practice called "penance." Penance included being truly sorry for sins, confessing these sins to a priest, and having the priest forgive the guilt of the sins and eternal punishment due them. It also included doing good works ordered by the priest. These works were done to prove the confession and sorrow sincere and to earn forgiveness for the temporal (earthly) punishment due the sins. The more good works a Christian did before he died, the less he would suffer in purgatory. Purgatory was a place for those Christians who had not done enough good works on earth. Here they would suffer the temporal punishment still due their sins before entering heaven.

Besides his own good works the Christian had another way to reduce his suffering in purgatory. The church taught that Christ and some saints had done more good works than needed. God kept these extra good works in a heavenly treasury, ready for Christians who needed them. However, a problem remained. How could the Christian get some of these extra good works for himself and thus reduce his suffering in purgatory?

This question the church answered like this: "Suppose you have confessed your sins, been forgiven, and are doing good works. Now, if you really want some of the extra good works in the heavenly treasury, you can earn them. For example, you can pray 'My God and my All,' or you can give money to help build a new hospital. In this way you will earn an indulgence. The indulgence will reduce the temporal punishment due you before entering heaven. God Himself will decide just how much to reduce your punishment and suffering in purgatory."

28

Normally the pope alone had power to give indulgences. But already in 1393 Pope Boniface IX appointed men throughout Europe to sell indulgences. To encourage sales, the church leaders wrote an "indulgence letter," which the pope signed and sealed. A copy of this letter, which promised forgiveness of the temporal punishment due sins, was given to each person who bought an indulgence. Thus the buyer had "proof" that his sufferings in purgatory would be reduced.

In 1476 Pope Sixtus IV added another point to the teaching about indulgences. He decided that indulgences could be bought also for those already dead. Now a loyal daughter could free her dead father from the tortures of purgatory — if she had enough money, that is.

"For Sale Cheap: Indulgences!"

But now back to Archbishop Albert. After getting the pope's permission to sell indulgences in Germany, Albert appointed special salesmen. Among these was John Tetzel, a Dominican monk from Leipzig.

Tetzel had been selling indulgences since 1504 and was an expert at it. Two or three weeks before visiting a town he would send a helper to announce his coming. This helper would also draw up a list of citizens, showing, among other bits of information, how wealthy each was. A large crowd would be at the town gate the day Tetzel arrived. They would march with him to the town square, where Tetzel would hold his first service. During the service he would preach on "Hell," describing in frightening language the terrors to be suffered by the unbeliever.

From the square Tetzel would move to the largest church in town. Here he would hold a second service, this time preaching on "Purgatory." "You children," he would say, "do you not hear the terrible cries of your dead fathers and mothers? You husbands, have you no pity for your wives who are being tortured in purgatory? Can't you hear them calling, 'Rescue us! Help us out of here! Help us to reach heaven!'?" Next he would preach a sermon on "Heaven," showing how happy, peaceful, and blessed were those who lived there. By this time the people were ready to buy indulgences, both for themselves and for the dead.

And so the sale would begin. People would pay anywhere up to $300.00, and sometimes even more. The exact price usually depended on how important and wealthy they were. Those who had absolutely no money could also get an indulgence, provided they would pray and fast as directed.

When Frederick the Wise heard about Albert's scheme, and especially that Tetzel had been picked to sell indulgences in Saxony, he refused Tetzel permission to enter. Frederick did not want large sums of money to leave Saxony to support the rival Brandenburg family. Besides, Frederick had his own system of selling indulgences!

The week after All Saints' Day (November 1) was always a busy one at the Castle Church in Wittenburg. For then the thousands of relics that Frederick had collected would go on display. People would come long distances to see a thorn from Christ's crown, four hairs from Mary's head, pieces from Jesus' crib, a hair from Jesus' beard, a gold piece brought by the Wise Men, a stone on which Jesus had stood to ascend to heaven, and bones of many saints. The people came because they believed that by seeing these relics and by making the proper contributions the pope would give them an indulgence — and that would greatly reduce their sufferings in purgatory.

The Hammer Sounds

All this concern for relics and indulgences bothered Luther. As pastor of St. Mary's Church he was responsible for his people's spiritual welfare. Therefore already in 1516 he had preached three sermons warning the people not to put too much trust in indulgences. "True inner sorrow and repentance for sin is much more important than buying indulgences," he had said. Although Elector Frederick grumbled about these sermons, Luther refused to stop speaking. And when early in

1517 Tetzel set up shop in Jueterbock, a village about twenty miles from Wittenberg and just across the Saxon border, Luther's patience soon came to an end.

Many in Wittenberg went to Jueterbock to buy indulgences from Tetzel. They showed them to Luther, expecting him to overlook their sins and to excuse them from doing the usual good works. Some even believed that the indulgences forgave the eternal guilt and punishment of sin. This encouraged people to sin. "So what if we sin," they thought. "All we need to do is buy an indulgence, and all will be well."

Luther preached a strong sermon against Tetzel and his methods in February 1517. But this and other warnings had little effect on the people. Not until October, after Tetzel left the area, did the interest in indulgences die down. And soon November 1 would be here — the day when the relics in the Castle Church would be put on display once again!

"Something must be done!" Luther said. Following the custom of the day, he decided to bring these matters to the attention of the church officials by inviting his fellow professors to a debate. He therefore put his thoughts into writing. When he was finished, he had written ninety-five theses, or ideas. In them he objected to using indulgence money to build a great church in Rome, and to the pope's claim that he had power over souls in purgatory. The *Theses* also argued that religion was a personal matter between God and man, and that the Gospel of forgiveness in Jesus Christ was all-important.

Luther sent the *Theses* to a friend to be printed. Then on Halloween (Holy Evening), October 31, 1517, he took a finished copy and walked from his room to the north door of the Castle Church. Here he took the paper and, with a few hammer blows, nailed it to the door. There was nothing unusual in this action; it was the customary way to announce a debate. Nor was there anything unusual in the opening words of the paper now on the door: "Out of love and zeal for making the truth clear, the following theses will be debated at Wittenberg, the Reverend Father Martin Luther, Master of Arts and Sacred

Theology, presiding. He begs that those who cannot be present at the oral discussion will communicate their views in writing. In the name of our Lord Jesus Christ. Amen."

And yet within a few weeks the *Theses* had been secretly translated from Latin into German and spread far and wide throughout Germany. Countless people had Luther's name on their tongues, some praising him, some condemning him.

Little did Luther realize how forcefully he had pounded the nails that fateful October 31!

4. The Echo of the Hammer Blows

AFTER nailing the *Ninety-five Theses* on the door of the Castle Church, Luther returned to the monastery. Here he quickly wrote two letters. One went to Archbishop Albert of Mainz, the other to Bishop Schulze of Brandenburg. Both told of Tetzel's activities and urged that these activities be stopped. With each letter Luther included a copy of the *Theses,* asking that they be studied.

Rome Hears the Hammer Blows

After reading Luther's letter, Albert acted quickly. He sent the *Theses* to Rome with a request that the pope forbid Luther to do any more public preaching or writing on such matters.

Meanwhile Tetzel himself got busy. "I will have Luther burned and his ashes scattered on the waters!" he threatened.

Since Tetzel was a Dominican, he turned to his order for help. In January 1518 the Saxon Dominicans met and honored Tetzel with a Doctor of Theology degree. The Dominicans also sent a message to Rome, warning the church leaders about Luther's false teachings and suggesting that he be silenced. This action meant even more than Albert's, for the Dominicans held much power in Rome. The general of their order, Cajetan, was himself a cardinal and thus was very close to the pope.

The Roman Curia, that is, the officials who help the pope govern the church, moved carefully, however. Pope Leo X asked the general of the Augustinian order, Gabriel della Volta, to contact Vicar John Staupitz. "Tell him to silence Luther," the pope ordered. Since there was to be a general meeting of the German Augustinian order in Heidelberg in late April, many believed that Luther could be made to change his mind there.

Heidelberg was about 270 miles from Wittenberg. Luther and a friend left Wittenberg on April 11, traveling on foot. Almost two weeks later they arrived safely at Heidelberg. This surprised many people, for the Dominicans had warned that Luther would be killed, while others believed that Luther would be captured and taken to Rome.

The meeting itself was unexciting. The Augustinians generally received Luther well and listened carefully to his talks about what was being taught at the University of Wittenberg. They did not order Luther to stop preaching and teaching. But they did ask him to prepare a pamphlet giving more details about the points raised in the *Ninety-Five Theses*. Luther was to send this to Staupitz, who, in turn, was to give it to the pope.

Luther returned to Wittenberg satisfied that he was not alone in his fight for the truth. His fellow Augustinians offered him a wagon ride, and he gladly accepted it. He later wrote: "I went on foot. I came back in a wagon."

But Rome was not satisfied. Its ears were still ringing from the hammer blows on the Castle Church door.

Rome Takes Action

Luther had not been ordered to keep silent, nor was he. A few days after his return to Wittenberg he preached a sermon in which he said, contrary to the church's teaching, "Not every person who is excommunicated will be lost eternally."

But Rome was busy too. During the last days of May 1518 the Dominicans held their general meeting in Rome. They convinced the chief judge of the Curia that Luther could no longer be trusted. The judge therefore ordered Luther to appear in Rome for examination. Luther was to be there within sixty days after the order reached him. It arrived in Wittenberg on August 7.

However, on August 23 Pope Leo X put his signature to a document that made the earlier one seem mild indeed. This document flatly called Luther heretic, that is, a person who no longer believed and taught as the church did. It ordered Cardinal Cajetan, who was representing the pope at the diet, or congress, in Augsburg, Germany, to arrest Luther. "When you have Martin in your power," the pope commanded, "keep him under a safe guard till you hear further from us." Similar letters were sent to Frederick the Wise and to General Volta of the Augustinians.

Why this new order? Three messages that reached Rome during July and August give the answer. Some of Tetzel's Dominican friends had heard Luther preach his sermon on "Excommunication" in May. Shortly thereafter they forged two documents. One was a set of theses on excommunication, the other an attack on the Roman Curia. These the Dominicans circulated widely, claiming that Luther had written them. Cajetan showed the documents to Emperor Maximilian I in Augsburg. When Maximilian saw them, he became so disturbed that he immediately sent a letter to Rome asking the pope to do something about Luther.

Luther and Cardinal Cajetan

Clearly Luther's life was in danger. He could recant, or take back, everything he had said. This would satisfy the Roman Curia, but it would not satisfy Luther. For Luther believed that he had to defend the truth as he had found it in the Bible. What should he do?

Luther decided to turn to his prince for help. The day after he had gotten the order to come to Rome, he sent a letter to Frederick asking for help. The elector believed that Luther was being treated unfairly and decided to support him.

Fortunately for Luther, Frederick the Wise had much more power over the Roman church leaders than did most of the German princes. There were two reasons for this. Old Maximilian I, the Holy Roman Emperor, wanted his grandson, King Charles I of Spain and Naples, chosen as the next emperor. The pope opposed this, as did Elector Frederick. In fact, the pope would have been pleased to see Frederick himself on the throne. Again, the pope wanted money and men from Germany to fight the Turkish armies invading southeastern Europe. Most of the German princes did not want to send help. Frederick, however, was willing. Thus if the pope wanted to keep Frederick on his side, he would have to deal carefully with Luther.

Frederick got in touch with Cardinal Cajetan in Augsburg. He asked Cajetan to let Luther appear before a German jury rather than go to Rome. Cajetan suggested, in return, that Luther appear before him personally, promising that Luther would get a fair hearing. When the elector agreed, Cajetan wrote to Rome asking that his plans be approved.

Approval came shortly. Pope Leo agreed that Luther need not come to Rome but could go to Augsburg and meet with Cajetan. However, Cajetan was not to debate with Luther; he was simply to find out what Luther taught and then give him a chance to recant. If Luther did not recant, Cajetan was to condemn him as a heretic, but not to arrest him. Leo was not yet ready to anger Frederick unnecessarily.

With mixed feelings Luther left for Augsburg on September 26, 1518. Even though he had a safe-conduct pass from both Frederick and the emperor, Luther and his friends doubted that he would ever return alive. Yet Luther did not hesitate. He was sure that God would protect him. While on the way he wrote: "Let the Lord's will be done. Even at Augsburg, yes, in the midst of His enemies, Jesus Christ rules." Luther arrived in Augsburg on October 7. However, he did not see Cajetan until five days later, because he insisted that the emperor give him still another letter of safe conduct.

Luther had three meetings with Cajetan. During the first Luther humbly fell to the floor before the cardinal. Cajetan, in a fatherly way, took Luther's hand and raised him up. Then Luther said: "I apologize for not having come sooner, but I felt I had to wait until I had the emperor's promise of safe conduct. I also beg your forgiveness for any hasty actions I have taken in the past. I have come here ready to be shown from Scripture where I have been wrong."

But this is just what Cajetan was unable and unwilling to do. In fact, his first words were, "Brother Martin, I order you to recant." Luther, however, would not do so till shown his mistakes. Though Pope Leo had told Cajetan not to discuss the matter, Cajetan soon found himself arguing with Luther. Cajetan tried hard to keep his temper, but on the third day he could hold himself no longer. He shouted: "Begone! Either recant or don't come into my sight again!"

Soon after Luther left, Cajetan met with Staupitz, Luther's superior. The cardinal asked Staupitz to do what he could to make Luther change his mind. Staupitz talked with Luther and got him to write a letter to Cajetan. Luther apologized for having lost his temper during the meetings and promised to stop discussing indulgences if his enemies would do the same.

Stories soon began spreading through Augsburg that Cajetan was planning to arrest both Staupitz and Luther. Staupitz decided to leave immediately. Before he left, however, Staupitz released Luther from his promise to obey the rules of the Augustinian order.

Luther stayed on a few more days. During this time he wrote a letter to Pope Leo in which he claimed that Cajetan had not been fair with him. He also repeated his willingness to recant if he could be shown his errors from Scripture.

Finally Luther's friends insisted that he leave Augsburg. They awakened him at night, led him through a little gate in the city wall to a waiting horse, and saw him gallop wildly away. On October 30, 1518, he was back in Wittenberg.

Two Troubled Months

After Cajetan learned of Luther's hasty return home, he sent two letters, one to Frederick, the other to Pope Leo. Both letters reported on his meetings with Luther, and both called Luther a heretic. He urged the elector to arrest Luther and send him to Rome for trial, or at least to force him out of Saxony.

When Frederick showed this letter to Luther, Luther immediately published his side of the story. Luther also appealed for a general church council, to include church leaders from all over the world. Luther claimed that such a council was above the pope and that its decisions had more force. This action, however, put Luther in an even more dangerous position, for church law said that no one was to appeal to a church council unless he had the pope's consent.

Frederick the Wise needed real wisdom at this point. As a loyal member of the church he wanted to obey its leaders. At the same time he wanted to protect Luther, especially since the Wittenberg faculty supported Luther. Moving carefully, Frederick first asked the emperor to drop his fight against Luther, or at least to promise that Luther would not have to go to Rome for trial. Then he answered the letter Cajetan had written him. He said that he would not send Luther to Rome until Luther had been clearly and unmistakably proved a heretic.

Meanwhile Cajetan's second letter had arrived in Rome. With the letter, Cajetan had included his own opinions about indulgences. These the pope made into an official document, adding that any who taught differently would be excommunicated. Luther, of course, had been teaching differently.

A Man Called Miltitz

With Emperor Maximilian near death and the Turks still winning battles, the pope could not afford to lose Frederick's support. He therefore tried to get at Luther by bribing the elector. Leo chose his secretary, Carl von Miltitz, as a special representative to the Saxon court. The pope picked his spokesman cleverly, for Miltitz was both a Saxon nobleman and a relative of Frederick.

When Miltitz left Rome, he carried with him many documents and instructions. Among them were the pope's decree about indulgences; special indulgences for the Castle Church in Wittenberg, whereby each of the 19,000 holy bones would reduce a person's stay in purgatory by 100 years; and a "Golden Rose" for Frederick. To receive this rose was a great honor. The pope personally blessed it and gave the award only once a year to some Christian ruler.

Miltitz left Rome in mid-November, determined to bring Luther back alive — or dead. But when he reached Germany, he lost some of his courage. Too many people were on Luther's side, he found. As he later told Luther, "I wouldn't risk taking you out of Germany even if I had 25,000 Swiss soldiers."

After visiting Cajetan in Augsburg, Miltitz moved on to Altenburg, about sixty miles south of Wittenberg. Here he met with Frederick and his advisers. Miltitz quickly saw that Frederick had no thought of surrendering Luther to him, even if it cost him the prized "Golden Rose," as Miltitz had hinted it might. So he tried a different approach. He told Frederick that Pope Leo no longer believed Luther quite so bad as Tetzel and the Dominicans had made him out to be. Miltitz also ordered Tetzel to appear before him so that he could scold him. Tetzel refused to come, however, saying that he would not be safe in Saxony.

Frederick next arranged for Miltitz to meet with Luther. After two days of discussion Luther once more agreed to stop complaining about indulgences if his enemies would stop complaining about him. Miltitz, on the other hand, promised to write a favorable letter to the pope, asking him to appoint a German bishop to examine Luther's writings and to point out any errors in them. Any such errors Luther agreed to recant. After a pleasant dinner hour the two men parted. Luther described the parting this way: "We separated peaceably, with a kiss (a Judas kiss!) and tears — I pretended that I did not know they were crocodile tears."

Elector Frederick fully approved of the two decisions reached. He even had Miltitz contact the archbishop of Trier, who agreed to serve as Luther's judge. On his way back to Rome, Miltitz also stopped in Leipzig to see Tetzel. He accused Tetzel of living an evil life and of starting unnecessary trouble. Even some of Tetzel's Dominican friends began to turn against him after that. He was alone and deserted. When Luther heard about this, he wrote to Tetzel: "Don't take it too hard. You didn't start this racket. The child has another father." On July 4, 1519, Tetzel died.

Meanwhile Miltitz made his report to Pope Leo. This caused Leo to write a surprisingly friendly letter to Luther. Apparently Miltitz had not reported honestly, for the pope told Luther how pleased he was that he was ready to recant. Leo welcomed him back into the church and even invited him to Rome to recant, all expenses paid.

An Emperor Dies

Leo must have been happy to write such a letter to Luther, especially at this time. He had more important matters to attend to than arguing with an ex-monk from little Wittenberg.

For on January 12, 1519, Holy Roman Emperor Maximilian I had died.

A new emperor had to be chosen. The pope did not want Maximilian's grandson, Charles I of Spain, to be elected. Nor did he want Francis I of France to get the throne. He preferred one of the German princes, especially Frederick the Wise. None, however, would have been strong enough to remain emperor for long, and so finally Pope Leo switched his support to King Francis.

Since the seven electors generally favored Charles, the pope worked hard to line up support for his candidate. He promised Elector Frederick the Wise the right to appoint anyone he wanted to be a cardinal, if Frederick would vote the right way. Pope Leo mentioned no names. However, both Frederick and Luther wondered. Was Leo offering Luther the chance to be cardinal — the chance to be one of the pope's closest advisers, to be in the group from which all popes are chosen? Was Leo becoming so desperate that he considered politics more important than false teachings?

For all his efforts, Leo failed to get his way. On June 28, 1519, the electors, including Frederick, chose Charles I of Spain as the new emperor. (As king of Spain Charles remained Charles the "First," but as Holy Roman Emperor he would be known as Charles the "Fifth.")

This election did not, however, completely free either the pope or the emperor to proceed against Luther as they wished. Charles still had wars to settle in Spain. Besides, across the border the armies of Francis stood threatening him. The pope, on the other hand, had to gain control over Charles, the man whom he had rejected as emperor. And so for almost a year and a half Frederick remained the most important prince in eastern Germany — and Frederick was not ready to surrender Luther.

5. A Wild Boar
in the Roman Vineyard

LUTHER had promised both Cajetan and Miltitz, "I will keep quiet if my enemies do the same." But Luther's enemies fought on. And so before long Luther found himself fighting another war of words.

John Eck and the Leipzig Debates

John Eck, professor at the University of Ingolstadt, was one of the enemies who broke the silence. Eck was a brilliant man and an excellent debater. Luther knew Eck, and the two had been close friends. However, when Luther wrote the *Ninety-five Theses*, Eck attacked them and their author. Luther replied in strong language. So did Carlstadt, another professor at the University of Wittenberg.

Finally Eck challenged Carlstadt to public debate, a challenge which Carlstadt accepted. This challenge was really directed at Luther, for Carlstadt was only defending Luther's teachings.

The debate was held at the University of Leipzig June 27 to July 15, 1519. Duke George the Bearded, ruler of middle Saxony, was among those present. Four men represented Wittenberg: Duke Barnim, the university rector (director); Carlstadt; Melanchthon, a young professor of Greek; and Luther. Eck, of course, represented the University of Ingolstadt.

Carlstadt and Eck began debating on the afternoon of the 27th. Eck talked freely, seldom using his notes and books. Carlstadt, on the other hand, read constantly from the pile of books that surrounded him. In fact, he read so much that he put many in the audience to sleep. However, the secretaries who recorded what the debaters said soon noticed that Carlstadt was getting the better of the arguments. Eck, too, realized this. Therefore on the second day he asked that no books be permitted. Though the Wittenbergers protested, the audience supported Eck. And so the rules were changed.

Now Carlstadt regularly came out second-best. He was no match for Eck. Eck, encouraged by his easy victories, was eager to debate with Luther. Finally he got his chance. On July 4 two of Germany's greatest debaters met.

Luther and Eck argued mainly about the question, "How did the papacy [the church government headed by the pope] come into being?" Luther claimed that it was a man-made arrangement, that God nowhere in the Bible ordered the establishment of such a government. Other topics covered in the two weeks included purgatory, indulgences, and penance. In every argument the basic difference between the two men became clearer. Eck placed the Bible in a secondary position, the teachings of the church fathers (tradition) first; Luther did the opposite, accepting the church fathers only where they agreed with Scripture.

As a result of the Leipzig debates Eck became very popular among the people and in the Roman Curia. They looked up to him as a leader in the fight against false teachings. On the other hand, the debates strengthened Luther's convictions, especially his belief that the Bible is the only true guide in faith and doctrine. And the more strongly Luther believed this, the weaker was his chance of ever returning to the teachings of the Roman Church.

Support for Luther

Luther, of course, was not alone in his fight against error. Elector Frederick protected him when he needed help. Staupitz supported and defended Luther. So did the Wittenberg faculty, especially men like Duke Barnim, Carlstadt, and Melanchthon. There were others, too, who in one way or another sided with Luther in his struggle.

One of these was Desiderius Erasmus. Born in Holland, Erasmus studied, taught, and wrote in many of the important cities of Europe. He was much interested in the achievements of the ancient Greeks and Romans and became an expert in the Greek and Latin languages. In 1516 he published a Greek New Testament with a Latin translation. Luther often used these two Bibles in his work. But more important to Luther, Erasmus also fought for the right to speak freely, even though this meant opposing the church and its teachings. The spread of such ideas of personal freedom helped Luther greatly during these difficult years. However, Erasmus was never able to make a clear choice between the Roman Church and Luther, and thus he and Luther finally drifted apart.

Albrecht Duerer of Nuernberg, Germany's most famous living artist, was another who used his talents to help Luther. Duerer's paintings, woodcuts, and copper engravings were the talk of the nation. When Duerer heard of Luther and his teachings, he rejoiced. He wanted very much to see Luther and to engrave his portrait "as a lasting memorial of the Christian man who has helped me out of great anxiety." Duerer never did get his wish. However, after 1520 many of his works showed Luther's influence and helped many more people to understand Luther's teachings better. Death cut the artist's life short in 1528.

Several German knights, especially Ulrich von Hutten and Franz von Sickingen, also sided with Luther. They believed that Luther could help them in their own fight against the Roman Church. These men were especially angered at the pope's interference in their political affairs and at his methods for draining large sums of money from Germany — by indulgences, for example.

Ulrich von Hutten was an educated nobleman with a strong desire to unite Germany against the "Italian clergy," as he put it. After the Leipzig debates Von Hutten became one of Luther's strongest supporters. "My goods for him I will not spare," Von Hutten once wrote. "My life, my blood for him I dare."

Franz von Sickingen, Von Hutten's close friend, twice invited Luther to seek safety in his castles. Once he even promised Luther one hundred knights if the Elector Frederick should decide not to protect him.

The War of Words Continues

Such support gave Luther added courage to continue preaching, teaching, and writing. Especially writing. The more Luther's enemies attacked him, the faster Luther wrote. Even the printers to whom Luther delivered his writings could not keep up with him.

Luther published three important booklets between August and November 1520. He titled them *An Address to the Christian Nobility of the German Nation, On the Babylonian Captivity of the Church,* and *The Freedom of the Christian Man.* In these booklets Luther hoped to make his position unmistakably clear to all. Once they appeared, any real chance of reuniting Rome and Luther disappeared.

Luther wrote the *Address* because he had come to believe that the German princes alone could reform the church. The *Address* had three main parts. Luther began by attacking the "three walls" that surrounded the Roman Church. One by one he broke them down. The first wall was the idea that the pope and the clergy are above all earthly rulers. Luther argued that all people, including priests, are to obey their government, except when it orders them to break God's Law.

Luther next attacked the teaching that only the pope could explain the Bible correctly. God the Holy Spirit, Luther argued, gives each Christian the power to understand the Bible for himself. Luther insisted, however, that each person must develop such power by careful study.

The final wall that Luther destroyed said that only the pope could call a general church council. If the pope or his followers sin against God, Luther wrote, then any Christian, especially a ruler, has the right to see that such acts are stopped.

And the best way to stop such sin in high places, Luther argued, was to call a church council.

In the second part of the *Address* Luther complained bitterly of the Roman Curia's sins. "At Rome there is such a state of things that baffles description," he wrote. "There is buying, selling, exchanging, cheating, roaring, lying, deceiving, robbing, stealing, luxury, evil living, crime, and every sort of contempt of God." Thirty-two suggestions for reform and improvement concluded the *Address*.

In the *Babylonian Captivity* Luther compared the Roman Church to King Nebuchadnezzar, who had once held the Children of Israel captive in Babylon. He said that Rome held the church captive with seven chains. These chains were the seven sacraments: Baptism, the Lord's Supper, confirmation, ordination (of priests), confession and penance, marriage, and extreme unction (oil applied to a person near death). Luther then went on to say that only three of the seven — Baptism, the Lord's Supper, and confession and penance — were really sacraments, that is, means whereby God forgives sins. And even of these three, one was doubtful. For while Baptism had water and the Lord's Supper had bread and wine, confession and penance had no outward sign connected with it.

Of the sacraments rejected, ordination was perhaps the most important. The church taught that ordination makes a man a priest for life and places him between God and other men. Only a priest can teach God's Word correctly, and only a priest may properly distribute the sacraments. In other words, the church taught that the only way to heaven was through the work of especially ordained priests. But Luther disagreed. All men are priests, he wrote. When a Christian congregation chooses one man to serve as its priest, he is only doing what all have a right to do.

Finally, Luther pointed out errors in the church's teachings about the Lord's Supper. He urged that the people be given not only the bread but also the wine. He denied that the bread and wine are changed into Christ's body and blood and then "sacrificed" for the people's sins. Jesus, Luther said, sacrificed Himself only once, on Calvary. The bread remains bread and the wine remains wine, Luther argued. But Christ's body and blood are really present, assuring forgiveness to all believers who eat and drink the Sacrament of the Altar.

Luther wrote *The Freedom of the Christian Man* to go with a letter to Pope Leo. Miltitz, who saw that matters between Rome and Wittenberg were going from bad to worse, had urged Luther to write the pope a kindly letter. Luther agreed, and in his letter he assured the pope that he was not attacking him personally, but only the false teachings that Leo was letting stand. "I look on you less as Leo the Lion than as Daniel in the lions' den of Babylon," he wrote.

The tract itself described the freedom that a Christian gets through faith. Because of his faith in Christ, the believer is "a free lord, subject to no one." Yet the Christian who has been loved by God now wants to return that love. And so he willingly becomes "the most dutiful servant of all and subject to everyone."

Of the three documents the third was by far the mildest. But it was written and published when the time for mildness had long passed. For, as we shall see, Luther had been excommunicated.

Rome Takes Another Look at Luther

News of the Leipzig debates reached Rome shortly after Charles V had been elected the new Holy Roman Emperor. A few months later professors at the universities of Cologne (Germany) and Louvain (Belgium) issued a report on Luther's writings. Both schools agreed that Luther taught falsely, that he was a heretic whose writings should be burned.

Events such as these made Roman churchmen wonder. Had Miltitz really been as successful in quieting Luther as he had claimed? They ordered Miltitz to meet with Luther once more. This he did on October 9, 1519. But the meeting accomplished nothing. In fact, Frederick the Wise told Miltitz, "I have already arranged to take Luther to the next German diet in Worms, where the archbishop of Trier will hear his case."

In November Pope Leo called John Eck to Rome. And on January 9, 1520, the Roman church court met once more to consider the Luther problem. For six months it studied the case. Finally, on June 15, 1520, Leo put his signature to the court's report.

The papal bull, or report, began this way: "Arise, O Lord, and judge Thy cause. A wild boar has invaded Thy vineyard." The bull went on to list forty-one reasons why Luther should be condemned as a heretic and excommunicated — unless, of course, he recanted. It ordered all Christians to burn Luther's writings and warned them against giving Luther any help. As for Luther himself, the bull gave him sixty days to recant.

Thus after struggling with Luther for over two years, the pope was finally ready to excommunicate him.

The Bull Is Published

Pope Leo gave Eck and Jerome Aleander the job of publishing, or officially announcing, the bull throughout the northern countries: Eck in eastern and southern Germany; Aleander in the Rhine valley and the Low Countries. Leo also ordered Aleander to inform Emperor Charles V of the bull.

Neither Eck nor Aleander was happy about his assignment. And for good reason. They often met open opposition. In some places they had trouble publishing and organizing book burnings. At the University of Louvain, the same university that had condemned Luther, Aleander saw students throw accepted church writings into a fire first started with only Luther publications. Eck was so glad to get back to Ingolstadt that he placed a tablet in his church "in gratitude that he has returned home alive."

The bull reached Luther on October 10, 1520. At first he pretended that it was forged, that it was only another of

Dr. Eck's tricks. But he knew differently, and before long he had written a sharp reply titled *Against the Evil Bull of the Antichrist*.

In his reply, Luther defended himself against the forty-one charges made against him. He called on the pope to take them all back. If Leo did not, he would prove himself "possessed and oppressed by Satan" and the persecutor of Jesus Christ. "I will not take back anything charged against me," Luther continued. "As they have excommunicated me for heresy, so I excommunicate them in the name of the sacred truth of God. Christ will judge whose excommunication will stand. Amen."

The Sixty Days Are Up

The bull had given Luther sixty days to recant. These days were up on December 10, 1520. Luther had not recanted.

December 10, therefore, was the day on which Luther officially became a heretic. It was also the signal for all Europe to begin burning his books. In Wittenberg, however, somebody burned the wrong books!

Philipp Melanchthon arose early that morning and posted an announcement on the university bulletin board. It invited the faculty and students to gather just outside the east gate of the city, on the banks of the Elbe River.

By 9 A. M. a large crowd milled around a pile of wood, anxiously waiting for the program to begin. Soon one of the professors stepped forward to light the fire. Then students and professors, including Luther, fed the flames with books and pamphlets — books and pamphlets that supported Roman teachings.

Suddenly Luther got an idea. He stepped forward to the fire, drew a copy of the pope's bull from his gown, and threw it into the flames, saying, "Because you have destroyed the truth of God, may the Lord consume you in these flames."

The crowd sang a hymn, after which the professors returned home. But the students were not ready to return to work. They marched through the streets of Wittenberg singing and shouting. One carried an indulgence on the end of a sword. Another, riding in a farm wagon, carried a copy of the bull six feet long. Ahead of them walked four students singing a Hebrew funeral song. These activities lasted well into the next day, when the town authorities finally stopped them.

Now what? In the eyes of Rome, Luther was a heretic. This became doubly clear when on January 3, 1521, the pope signed a final bull excommunicating Luther. In it he declared Luther and his supporters to be unbelieving heathen. Pope Leo also demanded that Charles V declare Luther an outlaw, one whom any citizen of the empire could put to death without fear of being punished.

But both Frederick the Wise and Luther had appealed to the emperor for a hearing at the diet now assembling in Worms. And the emperor had agreed. Furthermore, Luther had widespread support throughout Germany. Any attempt to arrest and execute Luther would be a risky affair.

For these reasons the German church officials took no hasty action. They hoped that the coming diet of Worms would help solve the problem. And Luther, too, hopefully turned his face toward Worms. Having been forced to burn many bridges behind him, he prayed that the one at Worms could remain standing.

6. "God Help Me!"

CHARLES V, Holy Roman Emperor and Defender of the Roman Catholic Faith, was only twenty years old when Luther burned the pope's bull. Yet Luther counted on him for a fair trial. What kind of man was Charles? And how had he become emperor over so much of Europe? Before describing Luther's visit to Worms, these questions deserve an answer.

The Young Prince Charles

Charles was born in Ghent, Belgium, while Luther was attending school in Eisenach. His father was Philip the Handsome, son of Holy Roman Emperor

Maximilian I and ruler of Burgundy, Luxemburg, and the Netherlands. Philip had married Joanna, daughter of Ferdinand and Isabella, the Spanish king and queen who commissioned Columbus to explore the New World.

Philip died, and Joanna became mentally ill when Charles was six years old. This made little Charles ruler of Burgundy, Luxemburg, and the Netherlands. When his grandfather Ferdinand died in 1516, Charles became king of Spain, of the Spanish colonies in the Americas, and of parts of Italy. In 1519 his other grandfather, Maximilian, died. Now Charles added Austria and nearby lands to his rule. In the same year Charles was elected Holy Roman Emperor. This gave him control over the German states. Thus, at nineteen, Charles had become Europe's most powerful ruler.

What was Charles like? After his father had died and his mother had become ill, his Aunt Margaret came from Austria to care for him. Private tutors helped educate him. Charles was not especially handsome. An Italian who saw Charles at the age of sixteen said: "He had a good body, thin but well formed, and of medium height. His forehead was broad and clear, but his eyes bulged and stared; they looked as if they were stuck on and did not really belong to him."

From childhood on Charles liked to be by himself or with only a few close friends. He seldom smiled. He had trouble feeling comfortable in a crowd, a feeling that often caused him to speak slowly and even stutter.

However, Charles also had his strong points. When faced with making a decision, he usually took his time, studying all sides carefully. But once he made up his mind to do something, he did it quickly. He knew how to judge people and to get them to do what he wanted. He was loyal to his friends and advisers. To win the support of the different people he ruled, Charles imitated their customs. His wife, Eleonora, daughter of Portugal's king, considered him a kind and loving husband.

Emperor Charles V

Charles was in Spain when he heard that Emperor Maximilian I had died. The young man of nineteen wanted very much to follow in his grandfather's footsteps. So he made every effort to win the coming German election. However, Francis I of France also wanted to be emperor. So did Henry VIII, king of England.

For a time the seven German electors, including Frederick the Wise of Saxony, were the most popular men in Germany. Visitor after visitor came to them, each trying to get a vote for his candidate. Some of the visitors brought money to bribe the electors. Charles probably spent over ten million dollars in his election campaign, half of which was used for bribes. But his efforts paid off, for on June 28, 1519, the day after the Leipzig debates had begun, each elector voted for him. Thus Charles I of Spain became also Charles V, Holy Roman Emperor.

One year and four months later Charles was in Aachen, Germany, accompanied by four hundred soldiers and officers. They were there for Charles's coronation, for his crowning as emperor. On the morning of October 23, 1520, a long line of people moved into the great cathedral. The archbishop of Cologne, representing both the church and the German people, asked the kneeling Charles, "Do you swear to preserve the ancient Christian faith?"

"I will," promised the emperor-to-be.

More questions followed: "Do you swear to protect the Roman Catholic Church? . . . to govern justly? . . . to guard the empire's rights? . . . to care for widows and orphans? . . . to honor your father in God, the pope?"

To each Charles agreed.

Then the archbishop turned to the congregation: "Do you promise to be obedient to Charles, your prince and lord, as the apostle Paul [Romans 13:5-7] has commanded you?"

Joyfully the crowd shouted its answer: "Let it be done! Let it be done! Let it be done!"

Next the archbishop anointed Charles with oil. This done, Charles stood up, put on his royal robes, and accepted the crown from the archbishop. Only then did he walk over and seat himself on the throne, the same throne used by Charles the Great (Charlemagne) over seven centuries before.

Germany had a new emperor, one that gave her new hope. Even Luther, as he wrote his *Address to the Christian Nobility of the German Nation* that year, believed that the young prince would bring peace to Germany, religious and otherwise. But the Diet of Worms quickly crushed all such hopes.

Charles' Crown Grows Heavy

"Uneasy lies the head that wears a crown." As king of Spain Charles had already learned the truth of this proverb. But as Holy Roman Emperor his head became even more uneasy.

The Diet, or congress, of Worms was scheduled to open late in January 1521. Here Charles would meet his first real test as emperor. Five problems had to be dealt with. First of all, Charles wanted to make his coronation official by having the pope bless him in Rome. For this he needed money, money which he expected the German princes to vote him. Again, Charles had Francis I of France to keep in check. And for this he needed both money and soldiers.

But the German princes expected something of their emperor too. Because Charles would be absent from Germany for long periods, they wanted to appoint a council that could rule when he was gone. The princes also had a list of complaints against the pope. They had presented this list to his grandfather Maximilian I time and time again, but without success. Now Charles was to be given the list, and he would be expected to see that the complaints were taken care of.

60

And then last, but by no means least, there was the Luther problem, a problem that both Rome and Germany expected Charles to help settle.

The Tug-of-War

Even before his coronation Charles had heard much about Luther. Pope Leo X had sent Aleander to represent him at the coronation and at the Diet of Worms. From the beginning, Aleander urged Charles to declare Luther a heretic and an outlaw. But Luther's supporters were also busy. Erasmus openly made fun of the bull condemning Luther. Von Hutten and Von Sickingen promised Luther protection. Frederick the Wise, too, fought hard for Luther.

Four of these men — Charles, Aleander, Erasmus, and Frederick — were in Cologne in late October and early November 1520. Aleander urged Frederick to let the pope handle Luther. Frederick, however, did not listen. He first met with Erasmus, who told him, "Luther has 'sinned' in two ways: he has attacked the pope's crown and the stomachs of the monks!"

Next the elector met with the emperor. Frederick reminded Charles: "When you signed the constitution of the empire, you agreed that no German would be taken out of Germany for trial. You also agreed that no citizen would be made an outlaw unless there was a good reason and unless he was given a fair hearing. And Martin Luther is a German." Charles promised to give Luther a fair hearing, and on November 28 he sent the elector a letter inviting Luther to appear before the Diet of Worms.

This was almost too much for Aleander. And the unfriendly reception he got when he entered Worms did not make him any happier. As he walked along the streets, people hissed at him and reached for their swords. Poems making fun of him appeared all over the city. All the bookstores had Luther's picture and writings for sale. No wonder Aleander feared for his life and wrote the pope, "Nine tenths of the people are shouting, 'Luther!' and the other tenth shouts, 'Down with the pope!'"

Aleander got in touch with Charles shortly after the emperor arrived in Worms. He told Charles, "Luther has no right to a hearing before anyone but Pope Leo."

Fortunately for Aleander, the news of Luther burning the pope's bull and Roman books angered Charles. So did a copy of Luther's *On the Babylonian Captivity of the Church*. Finally, on December 17, 1520, Charles changed his mind. He withdrew his earlier invitation to Luther. "Frederick can come to Worms," he said, "but he can't bring Luther!"

Now Aleander swung into action. He urged the emperor to issue an order making Luther an outlaw, to be captured or killed on sight. He even prepared one for Charles to sign. But Charles refused to sign without the diet's approval.

Meanwhile Frederick had another meeting with Charles. Once more he convinced the emperor to consider Luther's case. Shortly thereafter Charles appointed a committee of the diet to study the matter. But the committee refused to act, even after it heard Aleander attack Luther.

Early in February Charles had a new edict, or order, ready to show the diet. On the 13th Aleander talked to the diet for three hours, urging that Luther and his writings be condemned. On the 15th the diet met to take action, and the action was so violent that Frederick and the elector of Brandenburg had to be restrained from attacking one another! Finally, on February 19, 1521, the diet ordered Luther to come to Worms. It promised to examine Luther and give him a chance to recant his writings — but not to argue! If he recanted, all would be well; if not, the emperor's edict would be voted.

So Charles had to invite Luther after all. On March 6 he addressed a letter to "Our noble, dear, and esteemed Martin Luther"! Twenty days later the emperor's herald, or messenger, rode into Wittenberg and delivered the letter to Luther. Luther read it and made up his mind to go. He later wrote: "Unless I am held back by force, or Caesar [Charles V] takes back his invitation, I will enter Worms under the banner of Christ against the gates of hell."

On to Worms!

Luther, accompanied by the herald and three friends, left Wittenberg in a three-horse carriage on April 2, 1521. Between Wittenberg and Worms lay three hundred miles, each one bringing Luther closer to a possible death.

Yet the trip itself looked like anything but a death march. All along the way admirers crowded around Luther's carriage. In Leipzig and Naumburg Luther was the guest of honor. When Luther got to Weimar, he found out that Charles V had outlawed all his books. His friends begged him to return to Wittenberg, but Luther refused. In Erfurt, where he had studied and first become a monk, he preached to an overflow crowd in the cloister church. Luther preached again in Eisenach. On April 14 he entered Frankfurt on the Main River. Then on to Oppenheim.

Finally, on the morning of April 16, 1521, Luther and his companions neared Worms. A watchman in the cathedral tower saw them and announced their approach with trumpet blast. One hundred horsemen rode out to meet the travelers. When Luther arrived at the city gate, over two thousand people crowded around him. After making his way to his room he lunched with about a dozen leading citizens. Many visitors made the rest of the day pass quickly.

Luther Faces the Diet

The next afternoon the emperor's herald and marshal went to Luther's room. To avoid the crowds, they led Luther through a garden and through the back door of the bishop's palace. Here in a second-floor room the emperor, the electors, and the

German princes were gathered, waiting to see what Luther would do. Before long Luther stood face to face with his emperor.

The marshal spoke first. "Remember," he warned Luther, "you are not to speak except when asked a question."

Now the chairman of the meeting, John Eck, took over. (This, by the way, was not the John Eck with whom Luther had debated at Leipzig.) Eck greeted the emperor, the princes, and the clergymen. Next he turned to Luther. "Martin Luther," he began, "you are here by invitation of the emperor and the diet. You have just two questions to answer." Then, pointing to a pile of books on the table before him, he asked: "Do you admit that you have written these books? And do you defend them all, or are you ready to recant what you have said in them?"

Luther was just about to answer when his lawyer, a Wittenberg professor named Jerome Schurf, broke in to request, "Please have the titles read." This was done. In all, twenty-five titles were recited.

Now Luther was ready to answer, at least in part. "Yes, the books are mine; I deny none of them," he said. "But the second question I can't answer at this time. It has to do with faith and the salvation of souls and the Word of God. Therefore I humbly beg Your Imperial Majesty to give me time to think, so that I may answer without violence to the Word of God or danger to my soul."

Charles and the diet talked over Luther's request. Finally Eck told Luther, "Even though you don't deserve any special favors, the emperor in his mercy has agreed to give you twenty-four hours to think over your answer."

"God Help Me!"

Luther left the hall and returned to his room. Why had he not been ready to answer the second question? He realized that he would be confessing not only to the emperor, but to

God Himself. This frightened him. He wanted time to make doubly sure. And so he thought and talked with friends and prayed. Finally Luther made up his mind. Taking a pen in hand, he outlined his answer.

April 18, 1521, was a warm, sticky day. But almost every member of the diet was on hand for the afternoon session. In fact, so many came that a larger meeting room had to be found. Even then only the emperor and a few officials had room to sit. All Worms was excited, wondering what Luther's answer would be.

The marshal called for Luther at four o'clock. They walked to the bishop's palace. Luther, however, had to wait until six o'clock before entering the meeting hall. Finally, just as candles and torches were being lit, Luther was ordered brought before the diet.

Luther took his place. John Eck repeated the unanswered question: "Do you defend all your books, or are you ready to recant what you have said in them?"

This time Luther did not hesitate. "Most serene emperor, most noble princes, most merciful lords, these books are all mine, but they are not all the same kind. One kind deals with simple Christian truths about faith and life that even my enemies don't object to. If I denied them, I would be the only one of my friends and enemies to do so."

"Another kind," Luther continued, "complain about the false teachings and evil doings of Rome. They show how the pope and his followers are destroying Germany." Here the emperor broke in to object, but Luther would not be stopped. "No, I cannot deny these books, because if I did, I would be opening the door to even worse evils for my country."

And finally Luther came to the third class of books. "In these," he said, "I attacked certain persons whom I thought to be enemies of the Gospel. I admit that I may have used unkind language here and there. For this I apologize. But I can't take

65

back what I have said in defending God's truth. If I did, then sin and evil would increase their power. Show me from the Bible where I have taught falsely. If you can, then I will be the first to burn my books. Your Majesty, I put myself in your hands. Please do not let my enemies make you angry at me without a good reason."

Luther had finished. But had he really answered the question? The emperor, Eck, and a few other officials left the room to discuss Luther's words. They decided that he had not given a clear answer.

All talking stopped when the emperor and his advisers returned to the hall. Eck looked at Luther and said, "Martin, we are not interested in your argument about what the Bible does or does not say. Hus, Wyclif, and other heretics have always talked about this. What gives you the right to think you know more than all the popes, the church fathers, and the councils? I now ask you, Martin — and answer clearly and without any double-talk — do you or do you not recant your books and the errors in them?"

This was it. Luther had to answer. Beads of sweat appeared on his face as he began. "Since Your Majesty and your lordships want a simple, clear, and true answer, I will give it. Unless I am convinced by the teachings of Holy Scripture or by sound reasoning — for I do not believe either the pope or councils alone, since they have often made mistakes and have even said the exact opposite about the same point — I am tied by the Scriptures I have quoted and by my conscience. I cannot and will not recant anything, for to go against conscience is neither safe nor right. God help me! Amen."

A loud noise broke out in the room. Everyone seemed to be talking at once. Eck tried to restore quiet by telling Luther: "You cannot use your conscience in such matters. The teachings of general councils are far better guides." Luther started to argue. But Charles V had had enough. Excited and angry, he left the room. With that the meeting broke up.

Luther's friends crowded around and congratulated him. The emperor's Spanish friends, however, hissed at Luther and cried, "To the fire with him!"

When Luther finally got outside, he raised his arms in victory and shouted: "I am through! I am through!" Then he went to his room to rest.

One More Try

Aleander now urged the emperor to wait no longer. "Declare Luther a heretic and an outlaw!" he insisted. But Charles V did not want to act without the diet's approval. Therefore he met with the electors and some of the princes. Charles asked the men to issue an edict against Luther. But they hesitated, fearing that civil war might break out if they condemned Luther. Finally some suggested that another effort be made to convince Luther of his errors. A small committee was chosen to meet with Luther privately. Though the emperor refused to take part in the committee's discussions, he did allow Luther five more days in which to change his mind.

The committee and Luther met a few times, but got nowhere. The members begged Luther to accept the church's teachings and to recant his writings, but Luther always replied, "I will do so only if you can show me from the Bible or by clear reasoning where I have been wrong." Finally the committee realized that its job was hopeless.

Luther now saw no reason to stay in Worms any longer. He therefore asked the emperor for permission to return home. Charles gave him permission, together with a twenty-one-day safe-conduct pass — good only if Luther would stop preaching, speaking, and writing books that excited people. On the evening of April 25 Luther wrote a letter to the emperor and the diet. He thanked them for having treated him as best they could, and said he was sorry that all the meetings had been useless. The next morning he left in his carriage for home.

The Edict of Worms

Four days after Luther left Worms the emperor told the diet, "I am making plans to have Luther and his followers condemned." That evening Aleander sat down to prepare an edict. But when it was shown to some of the German leaders, they insisted that many changes be made. A new, approved edict of Worms was ready by May 12, but now Charles refused to sign it! Too much important business was going on in the diet. Besides, he did not want to stir up trouble just at this time.

But on May 25, 1521, Charles V could wait no longer. For on that day the diet would hold its last meeting. In fact, many of the members had already gone home, including most of those who supported Luther. So that evening he presented the edict to the remaining diet members. They approved it quickly. The next day Charles signed it, making it the law of the land.

The Edict of Worms called Luther a "devil in monk's clothing." It accused him of destroying the sacraments and of encouraging war, murder, robbery, and other crimes. For these and other reasons Luther was now to be considered an outlaw. No German was to have anything to do with him, except to capture or kill him on sight. His followers were to be treated in the same way. No one was to print, buy, sell, read, or own any of Luther's writings. No books were to be published that argued against the Roman Church or its teachings. Anyone publishing such books could be arrested and put to death, and his property would go to the one who had caught him.

There was no doubt about Luther's position now — at least so far as the emperor was concerned.

By the way, what had happened to Luther? Why had he not arrived at Wittenberg? Why had no one heard from him for almost a month? Why were people saying, "He's been murdered!"? And why were others saying, "No, he's been kidnapped!"?

To answer these questions, we will have to go back to the night of April 25, Luther's last night in Worms.

7. Kidnapped!

LUTHER heard the quick raps on his door. "Now who can that be?" he wondered. He walked over to the door and opened it. His tired face freshened up with a smile. "George Spalatin! How good to see you! Do come in." Spalatin hesitated. "Are you alone?" he whispered, his eyes searching what they could see of Luther's room.

"Yes," Luther answered. "But why do you ask? Is something wrong?"

By this time Spalatin had entered the room. "No, nothing's wrong. Not yet, at least. But it could be if Frederick's plan doesn't work. Come, friend Martin, let's sit down. We haven't much time."

So the two men sat down to talk: George Spalatin, secretary to Elector Frederick of Saxony, and Martin Luther, the Wittenberg professor who had dared to tell his emperor, "I cannot and will not recant anything!" Before long Luther knew why his friend had made sure that there were no stray ears around.

The Long Way Home

After Spalatin left, Luther began writing his farewell letter to the emperor and the diet. When finished, he turned to pack his few belongings. Finally he blew out the light and lay down on his bed. But Luther did not sleep well during his last night in Worms.

April 26, 1521, dawned none too early for the restless Luther. However, not till midmorning did Luther and a few friends, accompanied by the emperor's herald, leave Worms bound for Wittenberg.

But neither Luther nor the herald ever arrived in Wittenberg. Three days after leaving Worms Luther handed the herald a letter. "Here, this is an important message for the emperor and the diet," Luther told the herald. "Take it back to Worms at once." Soon the herald and his horse were only a cloud of dust in the distance.

Luther meanwhile continued his journey. By May 4 Luther's carriage was bumping its way through the heavily wooded Thuringian forest. It carried four riders: the driver; Petzensteiner, a Wittenberg monk; Luther's friend Nicholas Amsdorf; and Luther himself. As the hours slipped by and the late afternoon daylight began to gray, Luther became more and more nervous. His eyes darted from side to side, almost as though he expected a deadly enemy to appear suddenly from among the forest shadows.

And all at once five armed horsemen did appear. They galloped toward the carriage at top speed. When Petzensteiner saw them, he jumped from the carriage and ran. Luther, however, stayed in his seat. He whispered to Amsdorf: "Don't get excited. We're among friends."

By this time the horsemen were near the carriage. One of them reined his horse to a quick stop and dragged the sleepy driver from his seat. A second shouted, "Which one of you is Luther?" When Luther answered, the horsemen dragged him to the ground too. Worse yet, they shoved him into the woods and out of sight.

Amsdorf complained bitterly about this outrage. So bitterly, in fact, that the frightened driver never did catch on that the whole ambush had been carefully planned by Luther's friends. For Luther, who by this time was deep into the woods, was on his way to safety, not to death.

The Knight in His Castle

Luther, now dressed as a knight and on horseback, followed his captors through the dark forest. He rode for hours, growing more tired with each gallop. Shortly before midnight, Luther saw against the night sky the faint outline of a towering, hilltop castle.

Before long the band of horsemen halted in front of the castle, an ancient fortress known as the Wartburg. Once more the men grabbed Luther. They pulled him off his horse and shoved him into a room, locking the door behind them as they left. "Watch this man carefully," they warned the guard. "He's a dangerous criminal."

But they failed to tell the guard the "criminal's" name. This was all part of the plan, the plan which Spalatin had told Luther about that last evening in Worms. No one except a few trusted men were to know where Luther was being kept. Not even the Elector Frederick, who had worked out the plan, was to know. For Frederick knew that once the news of Luther's kidnapping began to spread, people would ask him, "Well, where have you hidden him?" And he wanted to be able to say, "Look, my friends, I have no idea where Luther is."

During the days that followed, Luther stayed in his room. Here he let his hair and his beard grow long and black, so that there would be less chance of anyone recognizing him. He also listened carefully to some of the knights who regularly visited him. He had a lot to learn before he could really play the part of a knight.

Not until several weeks later did the people in and around the Wartburg get their first real look at the stranger they had been wondering about. "Knight George, he calls himself," they said to one another. "Just who is he? And what is he doing here?"

In the Land of the Birds

In some ways Luther enjoyed his ten months at the Wartburg. His room was high above the ground, so high that he thought himself to be in "the land of the birds." From his window Luther could look out over the rolling countryside, green in summer; deep red, tan, and brown in fall; white in winter.

Luther would often leave his room for long, peaceful walks. But never alone. At least one attendant always went with him. Sometimes there were more, especially when a hunt was under way. Though Luther enjoyed the excitement of the chase, he could not help but feel sorry for any animal that might be killed. "Men who sick their hunting dogs on harmless little animals," he once wrote, "are just like the devil who sicks false teachers on innocent souls."

On one hunt Luther caught a frightened little rabbit alive. Instead of killing it, he wrapped it in his cloak and set it in some nearby bushes. Before he had gone very far, however, the dogs found it. They bit right through the cloth and killed the rabbit. This saddened Luther. "It's just like life in the church today," he reasoned. "No matter how hard I work, Satan and the pope continue to kill souls."

Luther had been able to scoop up only his Greek and

Hebrew Testaments at the time of his kidnapping. He therefore looked forward eagerly to visiting the nearby monastery at Eisenach. Here he was able to borrow armloads of books. How the monks must have wondered about this strange knight who thought more about books than he did about his sword.

Since few people knew where Luther was, he had few visitors. And even after some of his friends in Wittenberg found out about his hiding place, they did not dare visit him for fear they would be followed and Luther's life would be endangered. One day, however, Luther did have a surprise visitor: Lucas Cranach. The painter had brought along his canvas, paints, and brush. And while the two men talked, Cranach finished a painting of Luther. "Let's title it simply 'Knight George,'" Cranach said as he examined the finished portrait.

The Writer Writes Again

As Knight George, Luther carried a sword. But he never used it. For him the pen was mightier than the sword. And so, before long Luther was busy at his table turning out new books, pamphlets, and letters.

Luther welcomed the chance to write. Not only because it gave him a chance to dig more deeply into the Bible, but also because it made him feel useful again. Then, too, writing helped him to forget his loneliness and his sicknesses, at least for a while. Luther was not a well man. Years of hard work, little rest, worry, poor diet, nervous strain — these were beginning to leave their mark. Nearly all the while Luther stayed at the Wartburg he was bothered with digestive troubles and with sleeplessness.

Nevertheless Luther wrote. His first effort was a translation into German and an explanation of the 68th Psalm. He did the same with the 10th and 37th Psalms and with the Magnificat, Mary's beautiful song of praise and thanks for having been chosen as the mother of Jesus.

Luther also continued to write against some of the errors which had crept into the church. He had touched on the sacrament of confession and penance a year earlier in his *On the Babylonian Captivity of the Church.* Now he gave more attention to it in a booklet titled *Concerning Confession, Whether the Pope Has Power to Order It.* No person, Luther argued, should be forced to confess his sins to a priest. Especially not if he believes that only in this way will he be able to receive forgiveness. Rather, every Christian who truly repents and confesses his sins to God can be certain that he is forgiven, priest or no priest.

When Luther found out that some of the Wittenberg priests, monks, and nuns were marrying and leaving their monasteries, he decided to study the issue. The results of his study appeared under the title *On Monastic Vows.* Here Luther pointed out that many persons had become monks mainly because they believed that thereby they could better work their way into heaven. Those who did so were mistaken, however, for a monk is no holier than any other Christian. Besides, the only way to heaven is through faith in Christ and the forgiveness He has won for all men. For these and other reasons, Luther believed, no person should be forced to keep the promises he had made when becoming a monk, the promises to be poor and to beg, never to marry, and to obey strictly whatever rules were laid down for him.

But all these and other writings which Luther worked on during his months at the Wartburg cannot compare in importance with his translation of the New Testament into German. Ever since the fifth century the church had increasingly favored one Bible translation, the Vulgate. This was in Latin and thus was useless for the many who could read only their own native language.

Long before Luther's time certain learned men had made some translations into the language of their people. John Wyclif, a fourteenth-century English priest, spent many hours on an English translation. Several translations had also appeared in

Germany. The trouble was, these translations were either so poor or else so expensive that few Germans bothered or could afford to read them.

Luther determined to produce a translation that would speak the language of the common people. He decided to start with the New Testament. He worked steadily for three months, carefully making the Greek speak German, a German that the housewife, the butcher, and the baker could understand. He continued polishing the translation after his return to Wittenberg in March 1522. Finally he turned his handwritten pages over to the printer. And by September the first copies began coming off the press.

The New Testament sold rapidly, about 5,000 copies in two months. This is especially surprising because its price was high, about ten or fifteen dollars, a lot of money in an age when many a family earned far less than that in a month. The sales continued year after year. One student has estimated that nearly 300,000 copies were sold by 1546, the year Luther died.

Rumblings in Wittenberg

While Luther was busy at the Wartburg, his followers in Wittenberg were equally busy — perhaps too busy. With Luther away, some of them began taking matters into their own less steady hands.

There was Dr. Carlstadt, for example. Carlstadt was the professor and priest whom Luther had once rescued in a debate with John Eck. He set out to attack the rule that priests, monks, and nuns should not marry. Not only did he say that this rule was wrong, but he even went so far as to argue that a priest must marry. To prove his point, Carlstadt himself married a teen-age girl. And before long others began following his example, some leaving their monasteries to do so.

Carlstadt also worked to reform the church services, especially the Mass, or Communion service. On Christmas 1521 he stepped before nearly 2,000 people in the Castle Church.

He was dressed, not in the usual colorful garments, but in a simple black robe. In his sermon Carlstadt said, "From now on you do not have to fast and confess your sins to a priest before receiving the Lord's Supper."

Then he moved to the altar to prepare the bread and wine for distribution. Here he spoke partly in Latin and partly in German. How strange many of the worshipers felt! For the first time in their lives they were able to understand this part of the service.

Finally the preparations were finished. The congregation moved forward. One by one each person took a piece of bread and placed it into his mouth. But even more important, each person also was offered a sip of wine. Carlstadt had done what thousands of priests before him had never even thought of doing. He had given the people a complete Lord's Supper.

As could be expected, not all the people were prepared to accept such sudden changes. Many were troubled and wondered whether or not they were sinning by listening to Carlstadt.

Others, however, believed in Carlstadt. Thus when Carlstadt and a monk named Gabriel Zwilling began to preach against playing organs in churches or against placing statues and paintings in churches, trouble followed quickly. Mobs broke into churches and destroyed whatever they could lay their hands on.

Some of the same people also listened to and believed what the Zwickau prophets told them. The Zwickau prophets were three men who had come to Wittenberg from Zwickau, a village sixty-four miles south of Wittenberg. These men did not want children to be baptized, claiming that only adults who were able to understand Baptism had a right to it. They also claimed that God had talked to them directly. Therefore, they argued, they needed no Bible. In fact, nobody needed a Bible in their opinion. When God wants to tell people something, He sends the Holy Spirit directly. This makes even schools unnecessary.

Knight George Packs His Bag

The situation in and around Wittenberg was obviously becoming more confused every day. Young Philip Melanchthon, Luther's close friend and fellow professor, did not know which way to turn. He became so discouraged that he finally made up his mind to leave the university at the end of the 1522 term.

Frederick the Wise, too, wondered exactly what to do. He wanted to keep peace, and yet he did not want to stop anyone from doing what was in keeping with God's Word. He appointed a committee to study the Bible and to see what it said about some of the goings-on in Wittenberg. But the committee could not agree.

And when in January 1522 the Wittenberg town council passed a law which said that all the churches should distribute both wine and bread to the people and that all remaining images should be removed, Frederick was really on the spot. He finally put his foot down hard. Ordering the new law canceled, Frederick said that until agreement on changes could be reached, life in and out of the churches was to go on as it had been before all the trouble began. Not only that, Carlstadt was to do no more preaching.

But when the town council heard this, it acted quickly. The only way to straighten out this mess, the members agreed, would be to have Luther come back and again take over leadership. Therefore the council voted to invite Luther to return to Wittenberg at the earliest possible date.

When Luther received the council's invitation, he quickly made up his mind to accept it. Actually Luther had been in close touch with the situation in Wittenberg all along. His friends there regularly sent him long letters telling about the latest developments. Luther even tried to give some guidance to the Wittenbergers while at the Wartburg. His study *On Monastic Vows*, for example, was written for just this purpose.

In fact, Luther had heard and seen with his own ears and

eyes what was happening in Wittenberg. For on December 4 a dark-bearded, sword-carrying Knight George had secretly visited Spalatin, the elector's secretary. He had come mainly to find out why certain of his writings had not been published as he had ordered. However, he was also curious about how the Reformation was going. Luther was pleased that the people were being offered both bread and wine in the Lord's Supper. But he did not believe that anyone should be forced to take both against his will. Nor did he look favorably on those who were disturbing the church services or tearing down statues of Christ and the saints. "Preach and pray," Luther advised, "but do not fight."

In any case, Luther was ready to leave the Wartburg and risk a return to Wittenberg. And a real risk it was, for Luther was still living under the Edict of Worms. By this edict, you will remember, Emperor Charles V had made Luther an outlaw and had given anyone the right to capture or kill him on sight. When Luther wrote to tell Frederick that he was returning, the elector quickly sent a worried letter in return. Frederick reminded Luther about the dangers that he would face. "I will try to protect you," he wrote, "but I can make no promises. Therefore I wish you would stay at the Wartburg a little while longer, at least until I can be sure it is safe for you to come back home."

But Luther could not be stopped. He packed his few belongings. Then he walked out of his room and closed its door behind him for the last time. Once in the courtyard he paused only long enough to say a few last good-byes.

And with this Knight George mounted his horse and headed for troubled Wittenberg.

8. Work, Worry
and War

Nearly 150 miles, every one filled with possible death, lay between the Wartburg and Wittenberg. But Luther, still bearded and dressed in knight's clothing, galloped them away safely in five days' time.

A few people recognized Luther under his disguise. Or at least they thought they did. But after talking to Knight George about their discovery, they were no longer quite so sure.

The Black Bear Inn

Take, for example, the rainy night when Luther stopped at the Black Bear Inn in Jena, some fifty miles east of the Wartburg. After stabling his horse, he returned to the dining room. Here, in front of a crackling fireplace, he ate his supper, reading all the while.

All at once the door opened, letting in a gust of chill, damp night air. Two young men followed, their Swiss clothing mudstained and travel-worn. As the innkeeper spoke to them, Luther heard one say: "My name is John Kessler. My friend and I are on our way to the University of Wittenberg."

That was all Luther needed to hear. Waving to them, he called: "Come, please sit at my table. We will talk and enjoy our food together."

They hesitated at first. After all, a noble knight does not often call two strange students over to his table. But finally they came. And soon they realized that this was no ordinary knight.

For one thing, his talk. Instead of boasting about battles, swords, and horses, Knight George talked about Christ, the Bible, and the church. And then there was that book he had been reading. Not very many knights would spend their supper hour reading the Psalms, especially not in Hebrew.

Finally, one of the students said: "As you know, we are on our way to Wittenberg mainly because we hope to see and hear Martin Luther. Can you tell us, is Luther there now?"

Knight George's eyes twinkled as he answered. "No, I am certain that he is not there now. But I know that he will be there soon. In any case, be sure to study under Philip Melanchthon. He is an excellent teacher of Greek and Hebrew. By the way, what do they think of Luther in Switzerland?"

"Well, some think the world of him," came the quick reply. "Those who do say that God is using him to uncover truth that has been buried for centuries. Others, especially the priests, claim he is a heretic, a false teacher, and a tool of the devil."

At this point the innkeeper called one of the students over to him. "Look," he said softly, "do you realize who that knight really is? I'm sure that he's Martin Luther."

But when the student excitedly whispered this news to his friend, the friend did not believe him. "You must have misunderstood him," he argued. "My guess is that he said, 'Ulrich von Hutten.' He's the famous German knight we've heard so much about."

Not until the next morning, just as Knight George was readying his horse for travel, did the students ask the question that had been on the tips of their tongues the whole night long. "Tell us," they asked, "are you really Ulrich von Hutten?"

The innkeeper, who was standing nearby, heard the question. Walking closer he interrupted to say: "Young men, I told you last night who this man really is. He's Martin Luther."

At this the knight laughed. "You think I am Von Hutten. And you think I am Luther. Who knows? Maybe I am really the devil."

Then, as he mounted his horse, the knight turned to the young men and continued: "When you get to Wittenberg, be sure to give my greetings to your countryman, Dr. Jerome Schurf."

"But who shall we say sends the greetings?"

"Just tell him, 'The one who is to come, he sends greetings.' "

And off Luther rode.

The Welcome Home

From Jena the road curved northeastward. Fifty miles more of hard riding brought Luther to Borna, a little village near Leipzig. Here Luther rested.

Finally, on March 6, 1522, a Friday, Luther rode into Wittenberg. Though he came still dressed as a knight, he no longer tried to keep his name secret. "Martin Luther has come back!" This was the message that traveled from one end of Wittenberg to the other in a few short hours, long before Luther had time to get settled in his old room in the Augustinian monastery.

Dr. Jerome Schurf arranged for a welcome-home celebration on Saturday. Many of the Wittenberg faculty turned out to honor their long-absent fellow professor. Suddenly the guests heard a knock on the door. One of the men walked over to open it. And in stepped two young men, the two whom Luther had met at the Black Bear Inn.

Almost at once they knew that the innkeeper's guess had been right. They *had* been eating and talking with Martin Luther, not with Von Hutten. When Luther saw surprise on their faces, he laughed. "Come here, my friends," he called. "Meet Philip Melanchthon, the professor I was telling you about."

Back to Work

But Luther had not returned to Wittenberg for a round of parties. He had come to help restore peace and quiet and order and to lead his followers in the building up of a church — a church made up of members who were one in God and who stood firmly, as Paul had once said (Ephesians 2:20), "on the foundation of the apostles and prophets, Jesus Christ Himself being the chief Cornerstone."

Already early Sunday morning Luther began to build. Stepping into the pulpit of the Town Church, he preached the first of eight sermons that week. In these sermons Luther touched on many of the troubles that the Wittenbergers were having, urging them to be patient, to depend on God's Word for instruction, and to avoid forcing anyone to do anything against his conscience. "I can drive no one to heaven with a club," he reminded his hearers. He hardly needed to add, "And neither can you."

Powerful sermons like these soon had their effect. Mobs stopped gathering in front of monasteries to make fun of the monks who still remained faithful to their promises. No longer did they swarm into churches to disturb the services or to tear down the statues of Christ. Priests could once again wear their colorful robes without fear of having the people complain about them. And the Lord's Supper was celebrated two ways: those who wanted to receive both the bread and the wine could do so, while those who wanted only the bread were also taken care of.

Furthermore, some of the men who had stirred up much of the trouble now decided to leave Wittenberg. Carlstadt, for example, accepted an appointment as pastor of the church in Orlamuende, a small village near Wittenberg. Here he continued preaching against the use of statues and music in churches. Later he also began to tell his people that Christ's body and blood are not really present in the Lord's Supper, and that infants should not be baptized. To show his congregation that he was no better than they were, Carlstadt refused to let them support him. Instead, he labored as a farmer. Matters finally became so unsettled in Orlamuende that the Elector Frederick ordered Carlstadt to leave Saxony.

The Zwickau prophets, too, left Wittenberg. But not before they had tried to win Luther over to their way of thinking. In this they failed, however. Just before leaving Wittenberg the Zwickau prophets wrote Luther a bitter letter. In it they called him a new pope and an enemy of the true religion.

Thomas Muenzer

Of course, by leaving Wittenberg, Carlstadt and the Zwickau prophets gained freedom — the freedom to teach as they saw fit, even if the teachings did not agree with what was found in the Bible. And Luther could not be everywhere to keep matters under control. Luther's successful stand against both pope and emperor had given courage to many other religious leaders — leaders who had lost their faith in the teachings of the Roman churchmen. These now came out into the open, leading thousands of people down all kinds of strange paths.

Thomas Muenzer was one of these. Muenzer had first met Luther at the Leipzig debate. In 1520, at the age of thirty, Muenzer became pastor at Zwickau, partly through Luther's influence. But here his strange teachings began to get him and his followers into trouble, so much so that the Zwickau town council ordered Muenzer to leave. This he did, wandering from place to place, winning people to his side wherever he went.

Like the Zwickau prophets, Muenzer taught that God spoke to men directly through the Holy Spirit. This, of course, makes the Bible unimportant and allows people to teach almost anything. Thus Muenzer could argue that no one, whether child or adult, needs to be baptized. He also could claim that God had chosen him to build a new society, a society which was to include only Christians whom the Holy Spirit had touched in some visible way. These Christians had a job to do here on earth. First of all, they were to share their possessions with one another. Then, too, they had the duty to attack any government that tried to halt their activities, and to kill any unbeliever who might get in their way.

Luther, of course, opposed Muenzer. Especially after some of Muenzer's "chosen people of God" began to burn down churches. In fact, Luther urged the Saxon princes to order Muenzer out of Saxony. "God has commanded you to keep the peace, and you must not sleep," Luther warned. The princes followed Luther's advice. Muenzer left Saxony in 1524, the same year in which Carlstadt was forced to flee and just as the Great Peasants' War was getting under way throughout Germany.

The Great Peasants' War

To understand what the Great Peasants' War was all about, we will have to back up in our story for a moment. The peasants, or farmers, had long made up most of Germany's population. The average peasant was uneducated and had very little freedom. He worked long hours, either on his own little plot of land or on that of his master. Often he and his family had only an earthen-floored, one-room hut to live in. All in all, a peasant's work was never done, and at the end of his life he had very little to show for all his efforts.

During the two centuries before Luther's time the peasant's life became even more difficult. Taxes increased, clothing and other goods grew more expensive, and some rulers even denied him the use of the woods for fuel and hunting, the streams for fishing, and the meadows for grazing his cattle. Many peasants were forced into slavery, or at least the next thing to it.

These conditions were bound to result in unrest. Sometimes hundreds of peasants would gather in front of their ruler's castle and quietly ask him for help. But sometimes they would do more than talk; they would fight with whatever weapons they could find — picks, axes, gunpowder, stones, fire. Such uprisings had taken place in Germany in 1502, 1514, and 1515. All three had been put down by the rulers, but only after much bloodshed.

For a few years the peasants remained quiet. But then they began hearing about Martin Luther, a monk who had dared to disagree with the rulers of both the church and the state. They also heard about some of the things he wrote and said. They heard, for example, about his pamphlet on *The Freedom of the Christian Man*. How they loved him for teaching that the Christian is "a free lord, subject to no one"! And for showing them that they all were priests, that they all were free and equal.

Unfortunately, many of the peasants forgot that Luther was talking about man and his relation to God, not about man and his relation to the government, to the cost of a shirt, or to the right to hunt deer. This forgetfulness caused Luther, the peasants, the princes, the priests and bishops, and much of Germany endless trouble during the mid-1520s. For in 1524 and 1525 the peasants decided to make another bloody try for a better life. And men like Andrew Carlstadt and Thomas Muenzer did little to help the situation.

The first disturbances began near the Black Forest in southwestern Germany. From here the flames of revolt spread like wildfire to all parts of Germany and Austria. Actually there was very little unity among the peasant bands. Each did much as it pleased. However, some of the peasants did get together to draw up a statement of their demands. This statement was known as *The Twelve Articles*.

The demands found in the *Articles* were mild. For example, the peasants asked for the right to appoint and, if necessary, to remove their own pastors. Again, they wanted the woods, streams, and meadows to be open to everyone. The peasants also wanted certain taxes reduced or dropped, and they demanded that poor land should rent for less than good land.

Luther Takes Action

When Luther read these *Twelve Articles*, he was pleased by the kindly way in which they were written. However, he did not agree with all of them. He was especially disturbed about the peasants taking the law into their own hands, something which he believed God had given them no right to do. "Bad and unjust government excuses neither revolt nor resistance to the government," Luther warned. "Do not make your

90

Christian name a cloak for your impatient, rebellious, and unchristian undertaking."

But Luther also had something to say to the princes. "You do nothing but whip and rob your subjects," he scolded. And why? "In order that you may lead a life of splendor and pride until the poor people can bear it no longer. The sword is at your throats, but you think yourselves so firm in the saddle that no one can unhorse you. This false security and stubbornness will break your necks, as you will discover."

Luther, in other words, saw wrongs on both sides, just as he saw rights on both sides. He, therefore, urged the peasants and princes to sit down together with a neutral judge, letting the judge decide what would be best for everyone. But this was not to be. Matters had gone too far. Mere words could not bring the bloodshed and cruelty to a halt.

Not even in Saxony. Thomas Muenzer returned to Saxony against the elector's orders and began to stir up trouble. He turned the peasants against Luther, calling him Dr. Liar, Dr. Pussyfoot, and Dr. Easychair. "On! On! On! he urged." "Spare not. Pity not the godless when they cry. Remember the command of God to Moses to destroy completely and show no mercy. The whole countryside is in commotion. Strike! Clang! Clang! On! On!"

When Luther heard about Muenzer's activities, he decided to travel about Saxony in an effort to restore peace. What he saw and heard frightened him. Saxony would be ruined unless something were done — and soon.

Early in May 1525 Luther wrote a long, angry letter to the Saxon princes. He titled it *Against the Murderous and Thieving Bands of Peasants.* Using the strongest possible language, Luther urged the rulers to fulfill their God-given duty and stamp out the peasant armies. "Let everyone who can, smite, slay, and stab, secretly or openly, remembering that nothing can be more poisonous, hurtful, or devilish than a rebel. It is just as when one must kill a mad dog; if you don't strike him, he will strike you, and the whole land with you."

And this is just what the princes did. When Muenzer gathered nearly six thousand armed men near Frankenhausen, the princes took up the challenge. Their armies met the peasants, surrounded them, and killed nearly five thousand. The rest were taken prisoner, only to be beheaded later. Muenzer himself escaped, but only for a while. The soldiers soon found him hiding under a bed in the attic of a nearby house. They dragged him out and later tortured and beheaded him.

With the battle of Frankenhausen the Great Peasants' War neared its end. Although there were still a few battles to be fought in different parts of Germany, the peasants had lost their will to fight. By June peace had returned to Germany. But it was a sad peace. Hundreds of churches, monasteries, and castles lay in ruins. And nearly 100,000 peasants and soldiers had lost their lives in battle or through torture and execution. If anything, the peasants who remained alive were worse off than ever before.

Moreover, many peasants lost their faith in Luther. Though his letter against them did not appear till after the last battles had been fought, the peasants blamed Luther for sending the princes and their armies against them. From that time on many peasants looked to other men for leadership.

At the same time Luther lost faith in the peasants, especially in their ability to govern themselves. This attitude played an important part in Luther's later efforts to organize the Saxon churches. For he turned over the leadership of these churches to the upper classes, not to the common people.

But before detailing some of Luther's work following the close of the Great Peasants' War, let us take a look at what was happening in the empire of Charles V.

9. Building
the Reformation

CHARLES V, you will recall, was ruler of Burgundy, Luxemburg, the Netherlands, Spain and her American colonies, Austria, and parts of Italy. He was also Holy Roman Emperor, an office that made him ruler over all the German states.

The Absent Emperor

As Germany's emperor, Charles had signed the 1521 Edict of Worms, the law which made Luther and his followers outlaws. However, Charles had never been able to get all the German princes to enforce this edict. One reason for this was that Charles left Germany shortly after the diet of Worms, and he did not return until nine years later. Most of these years he spent in Spain, busily directing a war against his chief enemy, King Francis I of France.

During Charles's absence the German princes held several new diets. At each the representatives of Charles and of the pope urged the princes to enforce the edict against Luther. This the Roman Catholic princes were willing to do, but not

those who favored Luther. And since both sides were about equally strong, very little happened. The diets held in 1522, 1523, and 1524 did little more than say to the princes, "Enforce the Edict of Worms if you want to — and if you can."

No diet was held in 1525 because of the Great Peasants' War. However, during these months the Roman Catholic princes of Germany grouped themselves into two leagues, one in the north, the other in the south. And in January 1526 Emperor Charles signed a peace treaty with his French enemy, a treaty in which the two rulers agreed, among other things, to wipe out Lutheranism and its allies. As a result, Charles ordered the German princes to get ready to enforce the Edict of Worms.

Two Diets at Speyer

When the Lutheran princes of Germany heard about Charles's plan, they, too, formed a league, the League of Torgau. The strength of this league, plus the fact that Charles was soon readying himself for another war with Francis, made a great deal of difference when the German diet met at Speyer in the summer of 1526. With Charles absent once again and the Lutheran princes determined not to give in, the attempt to enforce the Edict of Worms failed.

In fact, the Diet of Speyer adopted a rule which proved very favorable to the Lutheran princes. The rule was simply this, that during the emperor's absence each German state would control its own church affairs as it saw fit. As could be expected, those states with Roman Catholic rulers allowed only the Roman Catholic religion, while those with Lutheran rulers supported the cause of Luther and his followers.

Charles agreed to this new plan, though he did so unwillingly. Yet he could do little else, at least not until he had settled his arguments with France. This did not happen until three years later, by which time the Lutherans and others who opposed the teachings and practices of the Roman Catholic Church had grown stronger than ever before — so strong, in fact, that Charles's efforts to enforce the Edict of Worms were bound to fail.

The second Diet of Speyer, held in 1529, proved the futility of his efforts. Charles ordered the German rulers to cancel the law they had passed in 1526 and to enforce the Edict of Worms throughout Germany. But this was too much, even for some of the Roman Catholic princes.

However, the diet did make some changes. By majority vote it ordered the Edict of Worms enforced in all Catholic states. In them no Lutherans were to be allowed to practice their religion. Where the edict could not be enforced without bloodshed, both Lutheran and Roman Catholic teachings were to be permitted.

The Lutheran princes refused to accept such a rule. They argued that it was unfair and demanded that Lutheran lands should be and remain strictly Lutheran. "We protest before God and before men," the Lutheran princes declared, "that we and our people will not agree to anything in this decree that is contrary to God, to His holy Word, to our right conscience, and to the salvation of our souls."

Notice the word "protest." When the Lutheran princes used it, they meant it in the sense of "testify," or "tell what we believe." From that time on they were known as the Protestors, or as the Protestants. This name lives on today and is used to identify Christian churches which do not agree with the teachings of the Roman Catholic religion.

Visits to the Saxon Churches

That the Lutheran princes should protest against the action taken at Speyer in 1529 was only natural, for in the three years since the first Diet of Speyer many of them had taken steps to reorganize and strengthen the churches in their lands.

Saxony, the home of Martin Luther, is a good example.

After Elector Frederick died in 1525, his brother John took over control of the government. The new elector supported Luther even more than Frederick had. Thus when the first Diet of Speyer gave each prince the right to determine the religion of his land, John was ready to go to work for Lutheranism in a way that his brother had never been willing to do.

John began by ordering a thorough investigation of church affairs in Saxony. He had Luther prepare a set of instructions for those who would be visiting the churches and schools. By the time the first visiting teams went out early in 1528, each had a long list of what to look for.

What the visitors found was not encouraging. Many pastors and teachers who had left the Roman Catholic Church and who now called themselves Lutherans knew little or nothing about Luther and his writings. Worse yet, all too many were poor examples for their people; they gambled and got drunk as they pleased. Some did not even know the familiar parts of the Bible. In one village Luther and Melanchthon found a pastor who had trouble praying the Lord's Prayer and reciting the Apostles' Creed. In another the people complained that their pastor spent his weekdays brewing beer and his Sundays preaching to them about how he did it.

Like pastors and teachers, so the people. Luther himself wrote: "Alas, what a variety of misery I saw! The common people, especially in the villages, know nothing at all of Christian doctrine; and many pastors are quite unfit and unable to teach. Yet all are called Christians, have been baptized, and enjoy the use of the sacraments, although they know neither the Lord's Prayer nor the Creed nor the Ten Commandments and live like the poor beasts and senseless pigs." And again: "Conditions in the congregations everywhere are pitiable. The peasants learn nothing, know nothing, never pray, do nothing but abuse their liberty, do not confess their sins, do not receive the Lord's Supper — almost as if they had been completely freed from religion."

Dozens of Sermon Books

All this moved Luther to action. Because so many pastors were unable to preach even a simple Bible-based, Christ-centered sermon, and because Luther had come to believe the sermon to be a most important part of the service, he sat down and wrote dozens of them. Actually he had been doing this for years; now he redoubled his efforts. Soon Luther's sermon books were in use throughout Saxony and, for that matter, throughout much of Europe. Many a pastor, teacher, and layman found them a great source of comfort and help.

Two Catechisms

Luther's Small and Large Catechisms proved even more widely helpful than his sermons. Even today these catechisms, especially the Small Catechism, are used in homes, schools, and churches throughout the world. In them Luther put the three chief parts of the Christian faith which he believed every Christian should learn and know: the Ten Commandments, the Apostles' Creed, and the Lord's Prayer. To these chief parts he added explanations, each designed to help young and old, pastor, teacher, and layman, to understand more fully what the chief parts really meant. Luther also added questions and answers about Holy Baptism, the Confession of Sins, and the Lord's Supper.

Luther urged pastors to preach the Catechism, teachers to teach it, and parents to study and share it with their children and servants. He himself never stopped using it. "Whoever is able to read," he once advised, "let him, in the morning, take a psalm or some other chapter in the Bible and study it for a while. For that is what I do. When I rise in the morning, I pray the Ten Commandments, the Creed, the Lord's Prayer, and also a psalm with the children. I do so because I wish to remain familiar with it."

Worship and Song

Besides sermons and Catechisms, Luther also outlined new forms for the Mass, that is, for the church service in which the Lord's Supper is celebrated. For centuries much of the Mass had been in Latin, a language that few of the worshipers understood. Worse yet, parts of the Mass were not in keeping with the Bible's teachings. To mention one, the Mass included the idea that in the Lord's Supper the priest sacrificed Jesus anew for the sins of the people. Furthermore, the Mass allowed for very little active participation by the congregation. The choir, for example, did almost all the singing.

Luther changed much of this in 1525, when he prepared his *German Mass*. This order of service — which, by the way, the elector made official for Saxon churches in 1526 — kept what was good in the old order, but cut out what was not. It was, first of all, in German. It allowed for a longer sermon, to be followed by distribution of the Lord's Supper, including both the bread and the wine. Again, the new order called for the pastor to chant and the choir to sing, but it also permitted the people to sing hymns of prayer and praise.

At first congregational singing was not at all easy, largely because there were so few hymns that the people could sing. Luther therefore had to prepare new hymnbooks. He encouraged his friends to write words and music for new hymns, but when they failed to produce them fast enough, Luther himself got busy. Actually, composing words and music for hymns was nothing new to Luther. Already in 1524 he had published a hymnal which included twenty-three of his own hymns. Other hymnbooks appeared regularly thereafter, many containing the latest works of Luther's musical pen.

Some of Luther's hymns have lived on to this day. Protestants throughout the world still sing the powerful stanzas of hymns such as "We All Believe in One True God," "From Heaven Above to Earth I Come," "Dear Christians, One and All Rejoice," and, of course, the Battle Hymn of the Reformation, "A Mighty Fortress Is Our God." Luther's hymns continue to proclaim the great truths of the Christian faith, a fact which led one student to say, "Luther did as much for the Reformation by his hymns as by his translation of the Bible."

The Bible Speaks German

This brings us to another of Luther's contributions: his translation of the Bible. Not only did this translation help build up the Saxon churches, but it also furthered the Reformation throughout Germany and even influenced the development of the German language itself. We have already seen how Luther prepared a German New Testament while at the Wartburg. Shortly after his return to Wittenberg he gathered a group of learned men, and together they began to make the Hebrew Old Testament speak German.

Although Luther had finished the New Testament translation in three months, the Old Testament took about twelve years. There were two major reasons for the delay. First, at the Wartburg Luther could spend nearly all his time translating. In Wittenberg, however, translating had to take its place among a hundred and one other duties.

Second, Luther found the Hebrew much more difficult to work with than the Greek. Sometimes Luther and his helpers would spend two, three, or even four weeks to find the right way to translate a single word. While working on the Book of Job they once used four days to finish three lines. As for the Old Testament prophets, Luther had this to say: "We are now sweating over the prophets. Oh, what a big job it is to force the Hebrew writers against their will to speak German! They do not want to give up their Hebrew and speak in everyday German. It's just like trying to force a nightingale to give up her beautiful song and imitate the cuckoo's monotone."

But finally the nightingale did sing like the cuckoo; and the song was, in spite of what Luther said, beautiful. The first five books of the Old Testament were published in 1523, while

Joshua to Esther appeared shortly thereafter. Then, one by one, Luther finished the rest of the books. In 1534 printer Hans Lufft proudly handed Luther a copy of the first truly German Bible. It contained both the Old and the New Testament and was illustrated with colorful initials and woodcuts.

As the New Testament had been doing for years, so now the whole Bible spread throughout Germany and Europe. Many welcomed it eagerly and dug through its pages to find out for themselves what God had done for them. What one of Luther's enemies said about the New Testament translation proved to be equally true of the whole Bible: "Luther's New Testament has been so multiplied by the printers and scattered in such numbers that even tailors and shoemakers, yes, even women and the simple who had learned to read only the German on ginger cakes, read it with great longing. Many carried it about with them and learned it by heart, so that in a few months they proudly began to argue with priests and monks on the faith and the Gospel. Indeed, even poor women were found who debated with learned doctors. Thus it happened that in such conversations Lutheran laymen could quote more Bible passages from memory than the monks and the priests."

More and Better Schools

The German Bible, along with the catechisms and the hymnbooks, were widely used in the schools that sprang up throughout Saxony and Germany, especially after the visits to the Saxon churches in 1528. Many of these elementary and high schools, and also some colleges and universities, resulted from Luther's efforts in behalf of education, especially Christian education.

There had, of course, been schools of all kinds in Germany for many centuries. Luther himself, as we have seen, had attended some of them. However, most of these schools had one or more weaknesses, inadequacies which Luther called on the leaders of church and state to correct. Luther was wise enough to know that the Reformation could not succeed unless there were strong Christian schools ready and able to train children and young people to be God-fearing citizens of both church and state.

One weakness which troubled Luther was that so few children actually went to school. This was especially true for girls. Already in 1520 Luther had urged the princes to set up boys' and girls' schools in every town. Here the pupils could learn the Gospel, also how to read, write, and work their arithmetic.

Not everyone agreed with Luther, however: men like the Zwickau prophets, for example. Also some parents disagreed, arguing that they needed their children at home and that they could teach their children all they needed to know. But Luther had an answer. In his famous *Letter to the Mayors and Aldermen of All the Cities of Germany in Behalf of Christian Schools,* written in 1524, Luther reminded his readers that too many parents fail to teach their children, because the parents don't want to be bothered, don't know how, or don't have the time.

As for children not having the time to go to school, Luther had this to say: "My idea is that boys should spend an hour or two a day in school, and the rest of the time work at home, learn some trade, and do whatever is desired. They now spend tenfold as much time in shooting tadpoles, playing ball, running, and tumbling about. In like manner, a girl has time to go to school an hour a day and yet attend to her work at home. For she sleeps, dances, and plays away more than that."

Luther thought so highly of the need for teaching children that in 1526 he reminded Elector John: Government officers have the duty "to force the people to send their children to school, especially such children as are promising. For our rulers are certainly bound to maintain the spiritual and secular offices and callings, so that there may always be preachers, lawyers and judges, pastors, writers, physicians, teachers, and the like."

The poor Christian training given in many schools was a second weakness that troubled Luther. Once Luther questioned a boy about the Lord's Prayer. The boy even had trouble understanding what Luther was talking about. When Luther asked him to tell who the "Father" in "Our Father" was, the boy was completely lost.

Luther, therefore, worked especially hard to improve the religion teaching that went on in the schools. His Bible translation, catechisms, and hymns provided some of the tools. But he also continually fought a battle of words to keep people aware and convinced of the need for using these and other helps wisely.

And for giving teachers the support and the respect that they deserved. Thus in his 1530 *Sermon on the Duty of Sending Children to School* Luther had this to say about the Christian teacher: "A hard-working, pious schoolmaster or teacher who faithfully trains and educates boys can never be sufficiently rewarded or repaid with money. If I had to give up preaching and my other duties, there is no office I would rather have than that of schoolteacher. For I know that next to preaching, it is the most useful, greatest, and best. In fact, I am not sure which of the two is the better."

Luther's battle for better schools produced many victories. Already in 1530 he could write the Elector this happy note: "Boys and girls are growing up so well instructed in the Catechism and the Scriptures that it makes me feel good to see how young boys and little girls can now pray, believe, and speak of God and of Christ."

And the high schools and universities were no different. For out of them came a growing number of pastors, teachers, lawyers, writers, mayors, and others, ready to take their place as leaders in church and state, ready also to help build and spread the Lutheran Reformation — in Saxony, Germany, Europe, and later, throughout the world.

10. The Family Man

Among those who benefited from Luther's efforts to improve Christian education were his own children. Since 1525 Luther had been a married man, and as the years passed he became father to a growing family.

This may seem strange: Luther, a family man! The same Luther who had once insisted: "They will never force me to marry!" And who had argued: "No, marriage is not for me. It wouldn't be fair to the woman, for I may be killed at any time. Then, too, it would interfere with my work. Why, some people would even say that I started all this preaching and writing just so I could get out of my promise not to marry. Besides, I'm too busy; I haven't time for a wife."

But somehow Luther changed his mind. Changed it enough to take into his life the now famous Katherine von Bora.

Katie

Katie, Luther called her. Katie had been born near Leipzig in 1499, about sixteen years after Luther. Her mother had died when she was still a small girl. Her father had remarried and later placed her into a convent near Grimma, about fifty miles south of Wittenberg. There at the age of sixteen Katie agreed to become a nun.

For about seven years Katie tried her best to win God's favor through a life of prayer, hard work, and holy living. But even her best did not always seem enough. Katie often became troubled and unhappy. At such times she would go to her Aunt Margaret, who as abbess headed the convent. Aunt Margaret usually knew just what to say to chase away Katie's blues.

However, in 1522 something happened, something which was to change the lives of both Katie and Martin Luther. In that year the nuns heard that some of the monks in Grimma had left the monastery for good. They also heard about and even read some of Luther's writings, including those which pointed out that only faith in Christ saves, not following certain rules in a convent.

The news left its mark on certain of the nuns. Twelve of them, including Katie, sent a secret message to Luther in Wittenberg, asking for help so that they could escape from the convent. Giving such help could mean the helper's life, for the laws of both church and state forbade it and attached the death penalty to it.

The severe penalty did not stop Luther, however. He wrote to Leonard Kopp, a friend who lived in Torgau, halfway between Wittenberg and Grimma. Kopp had a contract to deliver supplies to the convent near Grimma. Sometimes these supplies included herring. And herring came in barrels, each just large enough to hold a nun-sized person.

On the Saturday before Easter 1523 Leonard Kopp's creaking covered wagon, loaded down with fresh supplies, arrived at the convent. As usual, he helped the nuns unload the wagon.

No one noticed that he cleaned out the herring barrels more carefully than usual. When the unloading was done, Kopp slowly walked back to the wagon, checked to see that his horse was securely harnessed, pulled himself up to the driver's seat, and headed the wagon toward Torgau.

Shortly after nightfall he brought the wagon to a stop at the side of the road, turned, and stepped under the wagon cover. One by one he reached his hand into a dozen barrels and out of each helped pull a young, shivering woman, smelling just a bit like herring. "Strangest load of fish I've ever had," Kopp muttered through half-smiling lips.

By morning the wagonload of escaped nuns was in Torgau. Now what to do with them? Three returned to their homes. The other nine went on to Wittenberg. Here, with Luther's help, they found work, usually as governesses. And as the months passed many were married.

Not Katie, however. Although she was already twenty-four, well past the age when most girls of her day married, she was fussy. None of the men suggested by Luther and others appealed to her. None but Jerome Baumgaertner, a young man from Nuernberg who visited Wittenberg in 1523. The two met and fell in love. When Jerome left for home, he promised to return and marry Katie. But he never did. Katie was heart-broken. So much so, in fact, that she became ill.

Now Luther got busy. He wrote to Jerome and warned him: "If you want to hold on to Katie, you better act fast. Otherwise she'll marry someone else." The "someone else" that Luther had in mind was a Pastor Glatz. Katie, however, would have nothing to do with Glatz, no matter how much Luther tried to reason with her.

Finally Katie tired of Luther's arguments in favor of Glatz. She decided to visit Dr. Amsdorf, Luther's close friend. "Dr. Amsdorf," Katie said, "Dr. Luther is trying to make me marry Pastor Glatz against my will. Please ask him to stop. Tell him that I'll marry either you or him, but Pastor Glatz — never!"

When Amsdorf told Luther about Katie's proposal, Luther

laughed. Marry Katie now? In 1525, with the Great Peasant's War raging throughout Germany and the pope and Charles V still after his life? Ridiculous! Impossible!

Dr. and Mrs. Martin Luther

But in Wittenberg on June 13, 1525, the ridiculous and the impossible happened. For on that day Martin Luther, age 42, married Katherine von Bora, age 26.

Why did Luther marry Katie? Certainly not for love alone. Although Luther respected Katie, he hardly loved her in the usual sense, at least not before their marriage. Luther probably married Katie to prove that he believed what he taught, that marriage, even for a priest and former monk (and former nun), was God-pleasing. Luther also wanted to please his father, who had often urged him to marry to continue the name Luther.

Then, too, Luther felt sorry for Katie. He had helped her to escape the convent, but he had not been able to arrange a suitable marriage for her. Finally, Luther realized his own shortcomings; he needed someone to look after him. Maybe a wife would help him to eat and sleep at regular hours — and maybe even get his bed sheets changed regularly. "Before I married Katie," Luther later admitted, "my bed was not made for a whole year, and it became filthy. But I worked so hard and became so tired that I just tumbled into it without noticing the filth."

A man who didn't change his sheets for a year! What kind of husband had Katie gotten?

A Generous Husband

Well, she had gotten a man with a generous heart. Sometimes too generous for his own or his family's good. Luther always seemed to be handing out gifts. He emptied his pockets for needy students. One by one he gave away the silver and gold dishes that he and Katie had received as wedding presents.

Once a friend invited Luther to his wedding. Luther could not accept the invitation. He did, however, write a letter of congratulation. In the letter he promised: "I am sending you a vase as a present." When Katie found out that he planned to send away her precious vase, she took quick action. Luther was forced to add a P. S. to his letter: "I'm sorry about the vase, but I can't send it. Katie hid it."

But Katie could not hide the whole Augustinian monastery, which the Elector Frederick had turned over to the Luthers. Its doors were nearly always open. Through them wandered friends and relatives, students and professors, peasants and noblemen, rich and poor, Germans and non-Germans. Some stayed only for supper, more to listen to the Reformer chat than to eat.

Some stayed for months at a time — students at the University of Wittenberg, for example, who roomed and boarded with the Luthers. And some stayed for years, having no place else to go. People like Katie's Aunt Margaret, the former abbess, and the four orphaned children of relatives, whom the Luthers raised with loving care. Or like Dr. Carlstadt, who for years had been a thorn in Luther's side, but who now found shelter in that same Luther's home.

Add to these the Luther children (of whom we shall hear more below) and several family servants, and before long you have a busy, noisy household, one that cost a lot of money to keep going. It required more money than Luther had, but somehow or other Katie kept the household going. She managed the servants, the farm, the garden, the fishpond, the cattle. She even managed her husband, at least where money was concerned. For a man who could confess, "I don't worry about debts, because when Katie pays one another comes" — such a man undoubtedly needed managing.

Katie's husband was thankful for all this attention, even though he loved to tease Katie about it. As when he called her "my chain" or "my lord." Actually Luther just could not bring himself to worry much about money or about tomorrow. He

111

firmly believed that the Lord would provide, and the Lord did provide. Not the least of His gifts was Katie, the Katie whom Luther himself called more precious than the kingdom of France and the riches of Venice.

A Nature Lover

Yes, Katie had gotten a man with a generous heart. But also one who loved God's world and the treasures that it contained.

Simple treasures like a faithful dog. When Katie married Luther, Toelpel, Luther's dog, got his first mistress. From that time on he could no longer bed himself on the mass of papers in Luther's study, nor could he blissfully sharpen his teeth on his master's books, boots, and belts. All he could do was try, and then wait for Katie to pounce on him from out of nowhere.

Katie's husband also enjoyed puttering around in his garden behind the cloister. Here he tended his shrubs and fruit trees, his vegetables and flowers, especially his roses. "If a man could make a single rose," Luther once wrote, "we would give him an empire; yet roses, and other flowers no less beautiful, are scattered in large numbers over the world, and no one pays attention to them."

Flowers, of course, attract bees and birds. So Luther kept a few beehives and also took care that no one harmed the birds that made his garden a feeding or nesting place. Once Wolf Sieberger, the Luthers' handyman, set some bird traps. But Wolf put them away quickly after the birds sent Luther this protest:

> We thrushes, blackbirds, linnets, finches, plus other good and honorable birds, beg to advise you that we have information that Wolf Sieberger, your servant, has paid a high price for some old, worn-out nets, that he may rig up a trap to take from us our God-given liberty to fly in the air and gather grains of corn on the ground.
>
> Since this is very hard for us poor birds who have

no barns or houses, we humbly beg you to ask him to give up his plans until we have made our journey over Wittenberg.

If he will not do this, we hope that he may be repaid by finding in his trap, when morning comes, frogs, locusts, and snails instead of us!

The Music Man

One reason why Katie's husband took such good care of the birds was that they sang. Luther thought highly of any animal — or person — who sang. For he was a musical man.

We have already seen how hard he worked to help improve the singing of his fellow Christians. That he should prepare hymns and hymnbooks surprised no one who knew him well. Luther and music were inseparable.

Often when restless and tired, he would find a quiet spot and pluck the strings of his lute, humming the words of a hymn or a popular song. At other times he would gather his family and friends about him, and together they would sing away pleasant moments. Now and then someone would hit a sour note, but it did not matter. As Luther once wrote to a composer friend: "Even if all the world's governments were to punish us, and if God and reason were to write the tunes, nevertheless we would make such mincemeat of them as might be sold at the butcher's and make people wish us and our tongues hung as high as the church bells. You composers must not mind if we do make a mess of your songs, for we insist on trying them whether we fail or not."

Ups — and Downs

Generous, a nature and music lover, but also a man who could get depressed, angry, stubborn. Once Luther was unhappy for days in a row. Finally Katie could stand it no longer. So while her husband was out walking she changed into a black dress and practiced making a sad face.

When Luther returned and caught a glimpse of Katie, he became frightened. "Katie, what's happened?" he asked.

"Alas," she answered, trying to hold back the tears, "our dear Lord is dead."

"Nonsense, Katie. You know better than that. God lives, and He can't die."

"Are you sure, Martin? From the way you've been acting I was certain that He had died."

Martin Luther paused. Slowly a smile drifted across his face. He had caught the point. "You're right, Katie. I have no business being sad, for God is always the same loving God. I was wrong to go about acting as though He were dead."

But sometimes even Katie couldn't win her husband to his senses — at least not right away. Like one time when Hans, the Luthers' twelve-year-old son, disobeyed his father. Father Luther became so angry that he punished Hans as never before. For three days he refused to let Hans come near him, no matter how much Katie and others begged him to forgive and forget. "I'd rather have a dead son than a disobedient and wicked one," he argued. Finally, however, Luther gave in, and father and son were reunited in love.

Father Luther

Although he was a strict father, Martin Luther was also a loving one. God gave Martin and Katie six children. Hans came first, on June 7, 1526, just six days before his parents' first wedding anniversary. Then followed Elizabeth in 1527, Magdalena in 1529, Martin, Jr., in 1531, and Paul in 1533. The Luthers' sixth and last child was a girl, born in 1534 and named Margaret.

Not all the children outlived their parents, however. God called Elizabeth Luther home even before she had reached her first birthday. Both Martin and Katie were heartbroken. For a while Martin lost interest in eating and writing. "My little Elizabeth is dead," he wrote. "It is strange how sick at heart this has left me, so much do I grieve for her. I would never have believed that a father's heart could be so tender for his child. Elizabeth said good-bye to us in order to go with Christ through death unto life."

Fourteen years later the Luthers lost another daughter, Magdalena. Shortly before she died, Luther stood at her bedside, fighting back the tears. "Magdalena," he asked, his voice quivering, "would you like to stay here with your father, or would you willingly go to your Father in heaven?"

Magdalena looked up at him, trying hard to smile. Finally she answered, "Dear father, I'll do whatever God wills."

With this Luther turned away from her, but only for a short time. Magdalena's last moment had come. Kneeling at her bedside, his arms about her, Luther prayed: "I love her so much, dear God. But since You have chosen to call her away from here, I willingly let her go so that she may be with You."

Willingly he and Katie let her go, but they never forgot. "My dearest Magdalena has been reborn into Christ's eternal kingdom," Luther wrote to a friend. "Yet though my wife and I ought only to rejoice and be thankful at such a happy journey and blessed end, we cannot. So strong is our love that we must sob and groan in heart under the power of killing grief."

There were, however, also many happy moments for Father Luther. He played and prayed with his children. He listened to them laugh — and cry. Sometimes when they cried he would take them in his arms until the last sob had come and gone. Sometimes when they cried he became peeved, or at least he tried hard to make them believe he was peeved. Once, when one of the children started screaming because he hadn't gotten his way, Luther grumbled at him: "What reason have you given me that I should love you so, or that you should be my heir? None whatever! All you've done is made a nuisance of yourself and filled the whole house with your howls."

But Father Luther missed even the howls when he had to leave Wittenberg and home. On such trips he often wrote to Katie and the children. One of his most touching letters is this one to his four-year-old Hans:

Grace and peace in Christ, my dear little son.

I am glad that you are learning well and praying hard. Keep it up, my boy, and when I come home, I will bring you a nice present.

I know of a lovely, pleasant garden where there are many children. They wear golden jackets and gather rosy apples under the trees, and pears, cherries, and purple and yellow plums. They sing and skip and are happy. And they have pretty little ponies with golden reins and silver saddles.

I asked the owner of the garden whose children these were. He answered, "They are the children who like to pray and study and be good."

Then I said: "Good man, I also have a son. His name is Hans Luther. Couldn't he come into the garden, too, and eat the rosy apples and the pears and ride such fine ponies and play with these children?"

The man replied: "He may, just so long as he likes to pray and study and be good. His friends Phil and Justy may also come with him, and they will have whistles, drums, and fifes, and dance and shoot with little bows and arrows."

Next the man showed me a fine, large lawn in the garden all ready for dancing, where golden whistles, fifes, and drums, and nice silver crossbows hang from the trees all over. But it was still early in the day, and the children had not yet eaten. I wanted to see them dance, but I just couldn't wait any longer. So I said to the man: "My good man, I must go at once and write my dear Hans about all this and tell him to pray, study, and be a good boy, so that he may also come into this garden. But he also has an Aunt Lena [Katie's Aunt Margaret] whom he must bring along."

"That will be all right," the man said. "Go and write him about these things."

So, dear little Hans, work hard and pray well and

tell Phil and Justy to say their prayers and study, too, for then you will enter the garden together.

May God bless you! Give Aunt Lena my love and a kiss from me.

Your loving father,
MARTIN LUTHER

The garden, of course, is a child's vision of heaven, and the owner of the garden, God Himself. The letter — well, let's simply call it a striking picture of Martin Luther, the family man.

11. That They May Be One

LUTHER treasured Katie partly for her ability to manage their household so well. Because she was such a good manager, Luther could continue to give most of his time to the work of the Reformation and to its problems.

Among the more pressing problems was that of keeping the Protestants united. Ever since Luther's fame had begun to spread across Europe, many others had found courage to oppose openly the teachings of the Roman Church. But not all who spoke up agreed fully with what Luther preached, taught, and wrote.

The famous and learned Erasmus was one of these. So, too, was Dr. Carlstadt. Not to mention the Zwickau prophets, Thomas Muenzer, and others like them. And then there was Ulrich Zwingli, the religious leader of Zurich, Switzerland.

Ulrich Zwingli

Zwingli was born in Switzerland on New Year's Day, 1484, less than two months after Luther. His father, a government official, had him educated for the priesthood. At the age of twenty-two Ulrich took charge of his first church in Glarus, a small Swiss mountain town about thirty-five miles southeast of Zurich.

Here Zwingli spent ten years. Besides carrying out his priestly duties, he used much of his time to study the Bible. The more Zwingli studied, the more he began to wonder about certain of the church's teachings, especially those that disagreed with what the Bible taught. However, he kept his thoughts largely to himself, at least at first. But not for long.

120

In 1512, 1513, and 1515 Zwingli served as chaplain to the Swiss soldiers from Glarus. The pope had hired them to fight the French armies that were attacking Italy. When Zwingli returned to Glarus, he began to oppose the idea of the Swiss hiring themselves out to fight other people's battles. Not all agreed with him, and soon Zwingli found himself moved to Einsiedeln, a town halfway between Glarus and Zurich.

Although quite small, Einsiedeln was well known for a monastery which had been located there since the ninth century. Each year thousands of pilgrims from all over Europe visited the monastery church. Here they hoped to gain some special blessing from a black statue of the Virgin Mary — a statue reached through a doorway which promised that "here the full forgiveness of sins may be obtained."

Zwingli did not believe this promise, and he let his parish know it. He even urged several of the Swiss bishops to do something about this and other errors which had crept into the church. Among the other errors that troubled Zwingli was the sale of indulgences. For into Einsiedeln had come Bernard Samson, the Swiss John Tetzel, selling his letters of indulgence to help build St. Peter's Church at Rome.

In spite of his preaching Zwingli was appointed chief pastor of the cathedral in Zurich, one of Switzerland's larger cities. He took up the office on his thirty-fifth birthday, January 1, 1519. Almost at once he began to make changes, many of which he persuaded the Zurich city council to make into law. For example, the council forbade Samson to enter Zurich to sell the pope's indulgences. It ordered preachers to preach only what they could defend by the Bible. And in 1522 the council decreed that no one in Zurich should be forced to fast, except during Lent.

Now the Swiss bishops moved into action. They forbade Zwingli to preach. But like Luther, Zwingli had suddenly gone deaf, at least to such orders. Not only did he continue to preach, but he also published a book which clearly stated

121

that the Bible alone was the only perfect rule that a Christian could accept. Furthermore, Zwingli married, thus breaking one of the vows he made when he became a priest.

After this the Reformation gained an ever-stronger foothold in Zurich. And from Zurich it spread to other parts of Switzerland and even into southern Germany. Unfortunately, the teachings of Zwingli did not always agree with those of Luther. One reason was Zwingli's insistence that what the Bible says must always agree with man's reason, with man's ability to understand and figure it out. Luther, on the other hand, argued that the Christian must take God at His word and accept as true even what he does not yet understand.

Their differing approaches to God's Word caused much difficulty between the two Reformers and their followers. Especially troublesome was the argument that developed over the real meaning of the Lord's Supper. Both Lutherans and Zwinglians rejected the view held by Roman churchmen, that the bread and wine were actually changed into Christ's body and blood. Luther taught that while Christ's body and blood are truly present "in, with, and under" the bread and wine, the bread and wine remain bread and wine. Zwingli agreed that the bread and wine do not change. Such agreement was easy for him, since he rejected altogether the idea that Christ's body and blood are present in the sacrament in any way whatsoever. For him the Lord's Supper was merely a sign or symbol of Christ, no more than a rite which helped the Christian to draw closer to his Lord.

A Meeting at Marburg

Disagreement over the Lord's Supper came to be one of the main points discussed at the Marburg Conference in 1529. To understand why this conference was called, we need to remind ourselves of the second Diet of Speyer. At the diet the Lutheran princes had protested against the decision to allow

Roman Catholic and Lutheran churches to exist side by side in Lutheran lands. When a majority of the diet rejected the protest, the Lutherans and their supporters attempted to form a political union. However, not all the princes were agreed on matters of doctrine; some leaned toward Luther, others toward Zwingli.

Prince Philip of Hesse, a Lutheran, did not let disagreements discourage him. He felt certain that the doctrinal differences could be settled if only the two sides would get together and talk themselves out. Therefore he invited the German and the Swiss religious leaders to meet with him at his Marburg castle.

Most of those invited accepted. By the end of September the Marburg castle housed some of the most famous pastors and professors of Europe. Ulrich Zwingli and John Oecolampadius from Switzerland, Martin Bucer from Strassburg, and Martin Luther and Philip Melanchthon from Wittenberg were but a few of the famed theologians present. At Marburg some of the Reformers — Luther and Zwingli, for example — first met each other face to face.

The conference began on Saturday, October 2. Those present agreed to discuss mainly the Lord's Supper. Luther, sensing that this would happen, had prepared himself. He had chalked a circle on the table before him and inside the circle had written, "This *is* My body." These were the words Christ had used when He first celebrated the Supper with His disciples. Now Luther had his text, and Zwingli his target.

Back and forth went the arguments. Up and down went the tempers. The Zwinglians would say: "The *is* means *represents* or *stands for*. After all, Christ ascended into heaven, and His body is no longer here on earth." The Lutherans would reply: "The *is* means *is*. As the risen Lord, Christ can choose to be wherever He pleases."

Again the Zwinglians: "You mean to say that a sinful pastor can turn the Communion bread into the very body of the Lord?"

And once more the Lutherans: "Careful! We do not teach what you say we teach. The bread remains bread, but in, with, and under the bread *is* the body. Christ has said it and we believe it, whether we understand or not."

And so the conference continued — Saturday morning, Saturday afternoon, and Sunday morning. Finally, on Sunday afternoon most of those present realized that to go on would be useless. Luther thanked Oecolampadius for being so courteous and then turned to Zwingli, saying: "Please forgive me for any harsh words I used. Remember, I'm only flesh and blood."

Zwingli, too, begged Luther's pardon for any harsh words he might have used. To apology he added, tears filling his eyes: "I have always wanted to remain on friendly terms and still wish to. There are no men in Italy or France with whom I would rather be friendly than with you."

Although the conference was officially over, Prince Philip still had hopes for some kind of agreement. He therefore urged the two sides to prepare a statement of teachings which both could sign. On Monday Luther presented a fifteen-point statement, later called the Marburg Articles. All present accepted the first fourteen points, but not the fifteenth, which dealt with the Lord's Supper. Not until the following paragraph had been added did the Zwinglians sign the articles: "although we have not now agreed whether Christ's true body and blood are bodily present in the bread and wine, nevertheless each side is to show Christian love to the other as far as conscience permits, and both are to pray God that by His Spirit He would confirm us in the true understanding."

Because of the extra sentence, Philip's hope for a political union of those opposed to the Roman Church and its teachings failed. The sentence showed that the Zwinglians had "a different spirit," to quote a phrase Luther once used against Bucer. Although they parted as friends, both the Swiss and the Germans realized that each side would go its own way from now on.

The Diet of Augsburg

Thus when in 1530 Emperor Charles V issued a call for a new German diet to be held at Augsburg, the Lutherans had to face their enemies alone. As events were to prove, their strength and influence was great enough to gain them a hearing before the emperor himself. Even though the hearing was disappointing to the Lutherans, it did produce the famous Augsburg Confession.

Perhaps here we should say a word about the term "Lutheran." The first to use it were leaders of the Roman Church who opposed Luther's teachings. When they suspected someone of following Luther, they called him a *Luther*-an, that is, a person like Luther.

However, Luther and many of those supporting him did not want to be called Lutherans. They preferred to be known simply as Christians; or as evangelicals, people who believed and taught the simple truths of the Evangel, or Gospel. Already in 1522 Luther had asked "that men do not use my name and that they call themselves not Lutherans but Christians. What is Luther? After all, my teaching is not mine, nor have I been crucified for anyone."

As time passed, fewer and fewer people listened to Luther's objections. Certainly his enemies didn't; neither did his friends and followers. For they came to consider it an honor to be known everywhere as Lutherans.

Now back to the events of 1530. Not only did Charles call for the Diet of Augsburg, but he even planned to attend it himself. For the first time since the Diet of Worms nine years earlier Charles felt free to spend time on German soil. His wars against the armies of France and the pope were finally over. Now, he believed, the time had come to make one great effort to unite the Christian church. After all, with the Turkish armies threatening the gates of Vienna, Austria, it was no time for European Christians to be arguing with one another.

"Let us put an end to all disagreements," Charles therefore

urged. To help make this possible, Charles invited the Protestants to present their beliefs and arguments in writing and promised them a fair hearing. Not all the princes took him at his word, but John, the Elector of Saxony, did. He therefore asked Luther, Melanchthon, and others of the Wittenberg faculty to prepare a formal statement for the emperor and the diet.

By late March the statement was finished and handed to the elector at Torgau, a city some thirty miles south of Wittenberg. The Torgau Articles, as the statement came to be known, outlined some of the Roman Church's false teachings which the Reformers had worked to correct. These articles and several earlier documents, including the Marburg Articles, formed the basis for the Augsburg Confession, yet to be written.

In early April the Saxon representatives left for Augsburg. Included in the party were Elector John, Luther, Melanchthon, Spalatin, and many others. The travelers arrived at Coburg Castle on Good Friday, April 15. There they rested for a week, and there the elector broke the bad news to Luther — the news that Luther would not be permitted to go any farther, certainly not to Augsburg. For Luther was still an outlaw living under the Edict of Worms, and beyond the borders of Saxony there was no assurance that he would be safe.

Luther's Second Beard

Luther was badly disappointed. While he continued to hope that sooner or later he would be called to Augsburg, deep down he knew that this would not happen. This time Luther would have to let others fight the battles.

So Luther did the next best thing; he prayed and worked. He still had time to entertain many visitors. Some of his visitors were birds, whole flocks of them. This is how he wrote about them in one of his letters:

> There is a grove just under my window, like a small forest. There the crows are holding a diet. They fly in and out and keep up a racket day and night without stopping.

126

I have not yet seen their emperor, but their nobles and knights constantly flit and gad about. They are not clothed expensively, but all wear one color, all alike black and all alike gray-eyed. They sing the same song, but the voices of young and old, great and small, are different.

They care nothing for grand palaces and halls, for their hall has the beautiful, broad sky for a ceiling, lovely green branches for a floor, and the wide world for walls. They do not ask for horses or armor, having winged chariots on which to escape the hunter.

They are high and mighty lords, but I don't know yet what they are deciding. So far as I can learn, they plan a great war against wheat, barley, oats, malt, and all sorts of grain. Many a one will show himself a hero and do brave deeds. It is especially delightful to see in how knightly a fashion they strut about, polish their bills, and prepare for victory over the grain.

Others who visited Luther at the Coburg had no wings. There was John Frederick, the elector's son, for example. He tells us that by late summer "Dr. Martin has grown a heavy beard, so that if you met him unawares, you would very likely not recognize him." Just as at the Wartburg nine years before! Luther, you see, took the elector's advice to play it safe, even to the point of dating his letters "from the Solitude," or from "Gruboc" (read it backwards).

While Luther was at the Coburg, his father died. When Luther heard the news, he could not work for two days. He loved his father dearly. As he put it to Melanchthon: "It is my pious duty to weep for him whom the Father of mercy chose to give me birth — for him by whose labor and sweat God nourished me and made me what I am, such as that is."

The Augsburg Confession

Let us leave Luther mourning for the moment and return to the travelers on their way to Augsburg. The elector's party left the Coburg on April 23. One hundred thirty miles and ten days later the Saxons arrived in Augsburg, tired but still hopeful that the diet's results would be well worth their trip's hardships.

However, their hopes for a successful diet grew dimmer each passing day. Emperor Charles, still on his way to Augsburg, was acting strangely. He refused to let the elector visit him. He also forbade the Lutherans and other evangelicals to hold any preaching services in Augsburg. Then one day Melanchthon picked up a copy of John Eck's latest booklet, titled *404 Articles for the Diet in Augsburg*. A quick glance at the contents was all he needed to convince him that the articles submitted at Torgau would have to be rewritten.

What John Eck, Luther's opponent at the Leipzig debates, had done was to list all the so-called errors that he could find in Luther's writings. Eck made his findings doubly damaging by accusing the Lutherans of teaching doctrines which they actually did not teach. Doctrines such as Zwingli's regarding the Lord's Supper, or like those of the Zwickau prophets, who did not believe in baptizing children.

Melanchthon got busy at once. He spent hours on end writing, rewriting, and rewriting again. At times he became so discouraged that he broke down in tears. But he kept at it. Finally, on May 11, he finished the new statement and immediately sent it to Luther for examination.

At the Coburg Luther read it carefully. He nodded with approval when he saw how Melanchthon had handled his difficult assignment. Melanchthon had clearly pointed out what the Lutherans believed and taught and how they had tried to correct false teachings that had crept into the church. He had also showed clearly that the Lutherans did not accept the new errors of Zwingli, the Zwickau prophets, and others like them. And so Luther returned the statement, noting that "it pleases me very well, and I do not know how to improve or change it. Neither would it be proper to do so, for I cannot move so softly and lightly."

Though Luther was pleased with the statement — soon to be known as the Augsburg Confession — Melanchthon was not. He continued to revise it during May and June. In fact, he kept working on it until a few hours before it was finally read to the emperor and the diet. And by this time it had become much more than a Saxon confession of faith; it had gained the support of most of the German Lutheran princes, as their signatures proved.

The Emperor Listens

Emperor Charles arrived in Augsburg on June 15 amid the boom of cannons, the ringing of church bells, and the happy shouts of his subjects. He proceeded at once to a special service in the cathedral. In the evening Charles met with the Protestant princes and ordered them to stop their preaching services. They refused, and Charles lost his temper. He found it quickly, however, when one of the princes told him, "Before I would deny my God and His Gospel, I would rather kneel down here before Your Majesty and let you cut my head off!"

Charles replied excitedly, in his broken German, "Dear Prince, not cut head off! Not cut head off!"

Five days later, on June 20, the Diet of Augsburg began. Charles and the nearly twelve hundred noblemen representing all parts of Germany attended an opening Mass in the cathedral. From the cathedral they moved to the town hall, where the diet was to hold its sessions. On the first day little more was done than to announce the two big topics to be discussed during the diet: the Turkish threat and the religious differences that were splitting Germany, Europe, and the church.

During the next several days the Lutheran princes readied themselves to present their confession. For, after some argument, Charles had finally agreed to hear them out on the 24th.

However, when the 24th arrived, so did trouble. The session began late, at 3:00 P.M. Long speeches used up hour after hour. When George Brueck, one of Saxony's chancellors, finally gained the right to speak, the emperor cut him off with: "It's too late in the day to hear your confession. Why don't you just hand it to me? I'll read it and let you know my decision later."

The Lutheran princes protested. But Charles refused a second time. Once more the princes demanded to be heard. At last the emperor gave in. He announced that he would hear the confession the next afternoon. But not in the town hall. Rather in the bishop's palace, where only about two hundred persons could be seated.

The small room was filled to overflowing long before the emperor arrived. The air was charged with nervous excitement. At three o'clock the emperor took his seat on the throne. Shortly thereafter Christian Beyer, the other Saxon chancellor, began reading the confession in German.

Chancellor Beyer read for two hours, almost without stopping. He read so loudly and clearly that even those standing in the palace corridor and courtyard could hear him. Of course, two hours is a long time, no matter how well a person may read. Therefore every once in a while a head would nod wearily. Even the emperor had to fight to keep awake.

Finally Beyer came to the last sentence of the confession. "If there is anything that anyone might desire in this confession," it promised, "we are ready, God willing, to present more information according to the Scriptures." Then, after reading the nine signatures attached, Beyer stepped forward and handed the paper to the emperor's secretary.

At this point the meeting broke up, and the conversations began. The bishop of Augsburg, in whose palace the meeting was held, said: "It is the truth, the pure truth; we cannot deny it!" As if to support the bishop, five German cities at once added their names to the confession.

Prince William of Bavaria, a supporter of the Roman Catholic cause, turned to John of Saxony and admitted, "I've been misinformed about what you Lutherans really teach." Then he threw a question in John Eck's direction. "Dr. Eck, tell me, can you prove these teachings to be wrong?"

Eck thought for a moment before answering. "Well, I can if I use the writings of the church fathers. But not if I use the Scriptures!"

William was puzzled. "Do you mean to say that the Lutherans are sitting inside the Scriptures and we outside of them?"

The Emperor Decides

If William was puzzled, so was Emperor Charles. What to do now? Accept the confession as the truth and permit the Lutherans to teach and preach at will? Or condemn the articles and once more order the Lutherans to return to the pope's fold, threatening them with death if they refused? Yes, what to do now?

Charles turned to the Roman Catholic princes, priests, and professors for advice. At their suggestion he instructed John Eck and others to prepare a statement showing all the errors to be found in the Lutheran confession. By July 8 the statement was finished, all 351 pages of it.

But when Charles heard what had been written, he refused to accept it. "This will never do," he insisted. "Your hatred of the Lutherans shows up on nearly every page. Besides, it's much too long. Do it over again, and this time be sure that you answer the Lutherans with the Gospel and the Scriptures!"

Nearly a month passed before Eck and his committee could satisfy the emperor. But finally on August 3 the diet heard the Roman Catholic reply, now down to thirty-one pages. Although mild in tone and filled with Bible passages — many of which did not, however, prove what they were supposed to prove — the reply made one point very clear: The Lutherans had no choice but to give up most of their beliefs and return to the rule of the pope and the Roman Church. If they did not — well, the emperor would know what to do.

The Lutherans refused to accept the reply. Especially after they were denied a copy of it for study. Now Charles began to get worried and even desperate. He still wanted to win the evangelical princes to his side, for the Turkish threat was as great as ever. Already during July he had tried to win the Lutherans over by threatening them. Thus he and others had warned the elector of Saxony, "Either you agree with us, or you will lose your position and your land."

John, however, had remained firm. "I must either give up God or the world," he had said. "Well, there is no doubt about my choice. God made me elector — me, who was not worthy of it. I throw myself into His arms and let Him do with me what He thinks best."

Clearly, threats would not bring the Lutherans around. What then would? Charles decided to appoint another committee to study the differences. This time he chose fourteen men, seven Lutherans (including Melanchthon) and seven Roman Catholics. They met — and talked — and wrote, but got nowhere.

All the while the committee was meeting, Melanchthon did double duty. For he was also at work on a reply to the Roman Catholic reply. Chancellor Brueck presented this statement, later known as the Apology (defense) of the Augsburg Confession, to Charles and the diet on September 22. But Charles refused to accept it. Only a few moments earlier he had made an announcement which left no doubt that the Diet of Augsburg was over, at least for the Lutherans.

Charles had ordered the Lutheran princes, states, and cities to return to the Roman Catholic Church no later than April 15, 1531. While the Lutherans were making up their minds, they were not to print or sell any new books on religion, try to win others to their side, or prevent Roman Catholics from worshiping. This order was to stay in effect until such time as a general church council could be called to settle the matter once and for all.

132

The Lutherans Unite

And so the emperor's last great effort to reunite the Western Church had failed. Although the Diet of Augsburg continued till November, the Lutheran representatives left Augsburg almost immediately after the emperor announced his decision. The elector of Saxony and his party left on September 23 and headed for the Coburg, where they picked up Luther. By mid-October most of the Saxons, Luther included, had returned home.

If it had not been clear before, it certainly was now: Germany was a divided country, both religiously and politically. And any real hope of changing this fact had all but disappeared on September 22. Even the emperor's promise to have the pope call a general church council meant little. Few people believed that such a meeting, controlled as it was bound to be by Roman Catholic leaders, would accomplish much.

All this encouraged the evangelical princes to work twice as hard for unity among themselves. If Germany and the church could not be one, at least the princes had better unite. For unless they were united, a single armed attack by their enemies might well wipe out any gains they had made till now.

One result of their efforts was the League of Schmalkalden. Formed in February 1531, the league united many of the evangelical states and cities, each promising to come to another's defense if attacked. Largely because of his respect for the strength of the league Charles did not move against the evangelicals when they ignored his April 15 deadline.

Several years later, in 1536 to be exact, came the agreement known as the Wittenberg Concord. This agreement made Philip of Hesse especially happy, for it united the Lutherans and some of those who leaned toward Zwingli's teachings, especially regarding the Lord's Supper. While the Wittenberg Concord did not bring all the Zwinglians over to Luther's point of view, it did create a better understanding between the two groups.

Also in 1536 Luther began working on a statement for the

133

evangelicals to present to a general church council. Three years earlier Emperor Charles had been able to convince Pope Paul III that such a meeting was needed. Although the council was delayed year after year — it did not meet till 1545 — the League of Schmalkalden wanted to be ready. Thus, Elector John Frederick, who had ruled Saxony since his father John's death in 1532, asked Luther to draw up a suitable statement. This statement was to be discussed at a meeting of the league early in 1537.

The materials which Luther prepared were in many ways his last and greatest work. Later called the Schmalkald Articles, they were written at a time when Luther felt death was near. He therefore put his best into them. As he said when he had revised the articles for the last time: "These are the articles on which I must stand and, God willing, shall stand even to my death. I do not know how to change or to surrender anything in them."

And even to this day many Lutherans throughout the world still stand with Luther on these same Schmalkald Articles, just as they continue to confess with him, Melanchthon, and others the truths of the Augsburg Confession and its Apology. For these documents, like the church itself, are "built on the foundation of the Apostles and Prophets, Jesus Christ Himself being the chief Cornerstone." (Ephesians 2:20)

WHILE at Schmalkalden early in 1537, Luther suddenly became so ill that he had little hope for recovery. Melanchthon rushed to his friend's bedside. He prayed with Luther — and for him; he comforted Luther and gave him the best possible care.

During this visit Melanchthon and Luther spoke about many things, including the fact that a Christian needs to be ready to die at any time. Luther was ready, either now or later. "I am ready to die when and where God calls me," he assured Melanchthon.

But 1537 and Schmalkalden were neither God's time nor place. After weeks of suffering Luther passed the crisis and slowly began to mend. "Luther lives!" was the message that spread across Germany. And when some, especially his enemies, doubted that the message was true, Luther wrote a confession. "I assure you that I am still living," he began. Then immediately he added, tongue in cheek, "To the great disgust of the devil, the pope, my enemies, and myself."

Nine More Years

Actually Luther had nine more years to live. Nine more years in which to continue his fight for what he had come to know as the truth. And so, though he grew more tired and sickly with each year, he continued to read, write, preach, teach, pray, advise, and travel.

Even during these last years Luther never gave up hoping that the church would someday again be one. He refused to accept the idea that he and his followers had begun a new church. Luther insisted that all he had tried to do was to

138

return the Christian Church to the pure teachings with which it began. The simple Gospel truths, Luther argued, had been buried under layers of false teachings spread by those who had over the past centuries gained control of the church. If only a way could be found to convince these leaders that they had drifted away from God's Word! Or, if they would not let themselves be convinced, if only a way could be found to remove them from their seats of power!

Yes, *if*. Perhaps a general church council, such as that which Pope Paul III had promised, would be able to do the job. The trouble with a church council was, it would be controlled by the very people whom Luther and the evangelicals were fighting. And these people had a simple but unacceptable solution to the problem. "All you Lutherans need to do," they suggested, "is to agree that you are wrong and we are right. Then all will be well."

This hopeless situation led the League of Schmalkalden to refuse, not only once but several times, an invitation to send representatives to such a council. The first invitation came in 1537; the last in 1545, when Charles V and the French king finally forced Pope Paul to hold a church council in Trent, Italy. The Council of Trent was interrupted several times, so that it did not finish its work until 1563, nearly twenty years later.

By this time the German Protestants and Roman Catholics had fought several wars and had finally come to an understanding — not the kind of understanding, however, that Luther had really wanted. Both sides agreed that Germany would have two legal religions, the Lutheran and the Roman Catholic. Furthermore, each prince was to decide which of the two religions his state was to have. These decisions were reached, oddly enough, at another Diet of Augsburg, held in 1555. What they did was to repeal the Edict of Worms (1521) and put into practice the laws first adopted at the Diet of Speyer (1526).

But these events take us well beyond the nine years mentioned earlier. What else besides reuniting the church caught Luther's attention during his last years?

Philip's Two Wives

One of the problems was Philip of Hesse and his pair of wives. Philip, one of the leading evangelical princes, had married Christina of Saxony in 1523. He was nineteen at the time. During the next years six children were born to the unhappy couple. Unhappy, because Philip did not love his wife, and he made no effort to hide the fact.

When Philip later met and fell in love with seventeen-year-old Margaret of Saale, he made up his mind to marry her. But he faced a problem. He could not divorce Christina, because her father, Duke George, would not stand for it. Nor could he have the pope declare the marriage annulled, or ended. After all, Philip was a Lutheran. So he chose a third way. He decided to make Margaret his second wife. Philip figured this way: Abraham had two wives, and so did other Old Testament men. If they could do it, why can't I?

Christina, Margaret, and Margaret's mother Anna all agreed to the marriage. But Mother Anna insisted that Philip marry her daughter in a public ceremony. Also that Philip get some learned men to agree that having two wives was not against God's will. Philip turned to Martin Bucer of Strassburg for help. In 1539 he sent Bucer to Wittenberg to plead his case before Luther and Melanchthon.

Bucer did his job well. He returned with a long letter from Luther and Melanchthon which, in short, gave Philip permission to take a second wife. The letter also included this suggestion: "If your Grace should decide to take another wife, we think this should be kept secret." If for no other reason, one might add, than that bigamy (having two wives) was against the law.

Of course, Philip had already decided, and Mother Anna would not hear of any secrets. So before long the news was out. And all over Europe the enemies of the Reformation began shaking their fingers at Wittenberg and its two leading professors. Melanchthon became so worried about the gossip and the damage it was doing to the evangelical cause that he nearly died of grief. Luther, too, realized he had made a terrible mistake, though he did argue that Philip had not told the whole story when he asked for advice. In any case, Luther learned the hard way that a prince has no more right to two wives than does anyone else.

The Counts of Mansfeld

Some years later Luther was called to help settle another problem. It involved an argument between Gebhard and Albert, the brother counts of Mansfeld. Unfortunately the invitation came in midwinter and at a time when Luther's health was especially poor. Katie insisted that this was no time to take an eighty-mile trip from Wittenberg to Eisleben. "At least wait until spring," she begged.

But Luther would not listen. He felt duty bound to help settle the quarrel, which was hurting both the people and the work of the Reformation. So he made up his mind to accept the invitation and to forget all about the letter he had written to a friend only shortly before: "Aged, worn out, weary, spiritless, and now blind of one eye, I long for a little rest and quietness."

On the morning of January 23, 1546, Luther, his sons Martin and Paul, and several friends set out for Eisleben. Urged on by the biting winds, the party arrived in Halle two days later. Here the flooding, ice-choked Saale River blocked their way. While waiting for a chance to continue the trip, Luther visited with his old friend Justus Jonas.

Luther also took time out to comfort his worried Katie. "Dear Katie," he wrote her, "don't worry about me. Read your Bible and remember that God is almighty. He could create ten Dr. Martins if the old one were drowned in the Saale. Dismiss your cares, for I have One who cares for me better than you and all the angels can."

By the 28th the Saale had cleared enough to risk a boat trip across. After a rough but successful crossing the travelers once more headed for Eisleben. Before long a troop of 113 horsemen joined them. The soldiers escorted the party safely into Eisleben and up to the doors of the counts' quarters.

Now began a busy three weeks. Besides listening to the two counts and their lawyers argue, Luther preached four times, helped distribute the Lord's Supper, and took part in ordaining two pastors. Most of the time he appeared reasonably well, though he had to cut his sermon of February 14 short. "Much more might be said on this Gospel," he told the congregation, "but I am too weak. Let this be enough."

That same day, however, Luther wrote Katie an encouraging letter. "Grace and peace in the Lord," it began. "Dear Katie, we hope to come home this week if God so wills. God has shown great grace to the lords, who have agreed on all but two or three points. However, the brothers Count Albert and Count Gebhard still need to be made real brothers. I shall try to do this today and shall invite both to visit me so that they may see each other. For up till now they have not spoken to each other, but have angered each other by writing. But the young lords and ladies are happy and go partying and skating and have masquerades and are very jolly, even Count Gebhard's son. So we see that God hears prayer."

The Last Word

February 17 began happily. On that day the two counts settled their last differences and agreed to live peaceably in the future. Luther relaxed and looked forward to returning to Wittenberg and home.

That evening, after supper, Luther excused himself and went to his room to rest. Martin and Paul went with their father. Later several others, including Justus Jonas, joined them. All at once Luther complained of a pain in his chest, near his heart. Those present quickly called for the doctors.

142

The doctors applied hot cloths to Luther's chest and massaged the area to increase the blood circulation. Then, after giving Luther a dose of medicine, they carried him to the couch, where he slept for about an hour.

Luther awoke at ten o'clock. Surprised at seeing the visitors still present, Luther said: "Are you still up? Don't you want to go to bed? Well, whatever you do, I'm going to bed right now." With that he said good night, retired to his bedroom, and fell asleep almost at once.

Jonas and another friend stayed with Luther for the next hours. About two in the morning they heard a cry of pain from the bedroom. Rushing in, they saw that Luther had had another attack. "O my God," Luther moaned, "what a great pain! O dear Dr. Jonas, I believe I'll stay in Eisleben, where I was born and baptized."

Despite the pain, Luther got out of bed and walked into the next room. Here he sat down on the couch. While his friends worked to comfort him, Luther continued to pray, much as he had been doing ever since his first attack. "Father, into Thy hands I commend myself," he prayed. And again: "O my heavenly Father, one God, and Father of our Lord Jesus Christ, Thou God of all comfort, I thank·Thee that Thou hast given for me Thy dear Son Jesus Christ, in whom I believe, whom I have preached and confessed, loved and praised, whom the wicked pope and all the godless shame, persecute, and make fun of. I pray Thee, dear Lord Jesus Christ, let me commend my little soul to Thee. O heavenly Father, if I leave this body and depart, I am certain that I will be with Thee forever and can never, never tear myself out of Thy hands. God so loved the world that He gave His only-begotten Son, that whosoever believeth in Him should not perish but have everlasting life."

This was the last prayer that Luther ever prayed. Shortly thereafter he had a third attack, much worse than either of the first two. The doctors were called again, but they quickly gave up all hope. Sensing that the end was near, Justus Jonas stepped over to the couch and asked in a loud voice, "Reverend Father, are you willing to die in the name of the Christ and the doctrine which you have preached?"

"Yes!" came the answer, loud enough for all to hear. And with this final confession of faith Luther fell asleep. Asleep in Jesus, no less.

Laid to Rest

Martin Luther, age 62, died at about three o'clock the morning of February 18, 1546. Even before dawn arrived, many in Eisleben and the surrounding countryside had heard the sad news. Later in the day Luther's friends removed his body so that it could be readied for the funeral service. The funeral was held the next day in St. Andrew's Church, just across the street from the house where Luther had died. Justus Jonas preached the sermon.

A second funeral service was held early on the 20th. Then, about noon, several men carried Luther's tin coffin out of the church and placed it on a wagon. Soon the long trip back to Wittenberg got under way. Accompanied by a large escort of princes, soldiers, and friends, the funeral wagon slowly jolted its way along the rough road. Crowds gathered everywhere to honor the late Reformer. In Halle, where Luther's body was to rest overnight, people, horses, and wagons were so thick that the funeral procession had trouble even moving.

Finally, on February 22, Luther's body arrived in Wittenberg, on its way to the waiting grave in the Castle Church. Amid the tolling of bells, two mounted knights and sixty horsemen moved ahead of the wagon carrying the coffin. Luther's wife, his three sons and daughter Margaret and relatives and friends followed in carriages. Walking slowly behind came the teachers and students of the University of Wittenberg, the members of the town council, and many leading citizens. Long lines of common people, numbering in the thousands, completed the parade of mourners winding its way through the narrow streets.

Luther's body was carried into the church through the same door on which he had nailed the *Ninety-five Theses* nearly thirty years earlier. Inside, crowds filled the church to overflowing. Philip Melanchthon and John Bugenhagen reminded the mourners of the importance of Luther's life and labors. As the last echoes of the service faded, the Reformer's body was lowered into its final resting place under the floor in front of the pulpit.

13. In Death He Lives

MARTIN LUTHER, priest, professor, reformer, father, hymn-writer, hero of faith — Martin Luther was dead. As the word spread across Germany and Europe, many mourned with Katie and the people of Wittenberg, with those who had come to know Luther best.

Some, however, rejoiced. Now, they reasoned, we can quickly take care of Luther's disciples. For without a leader, the followers will not know which way to turn.

But those who reasoned thus were bound to be disappointed. For Luther continued to live on in the lives of those whom he had touched, both directly and indirectly. Already during his lifetime Luther had seen the evangelical cause gain hold in many lands besides Germany. Denmark, Norway, Iceland, Sweden, Finland were among the first countries to find Luther the man they had been waiting for. And from here and elsewhere Luther's teachings flowed down through the centuries into all parts of the world: into the Americas, into Africa, Asia, Australia, and even into the islands dotting the oceans.

The Power of the Gospel

What was the secret of Luther's teachings, of the fact that he and his beliefs could not die? The answer is, in a way, rather simple. Luther took God at His word and fearlessly told the world so. At the same time Luther refused to go beyond that Word. Therefore the Gospel which Luther preached, Christ's Gospel, became a power that not even the devil could resist.

Philip Melanchthon hinted at this when he preached at Luther's funeral. "Luther brought to light the true and necessary doctrine," Melanchthon reminded his hearers. "He showed what true repentance is and what is the true refuge and the sure comfort of the soul which trembles at the thought of God's anger. He taught Paul's doctrine, which says that man is justified by faith." To this one need only add: justified by faith in Jesus Christ, the world's perfect and only Savior, and apart from works of law.

Luther himself has left behind a striking picture which illustrates the secret of his power even more clearly. The picture is to be found in his famous coat of arms, or seal, which looks like this:

Luther designed this seal while teaching at Wittenberg. He wanted it to summarize his faith. It did just that, as his explanation shows:

> The first thing expressed in my seal is a cross, black, within the red heart, to put me in mind that faith in Christ crucified saves us. "For with the heart man believes unto righteousness." ✝ Now, although the cross is black, shameful, and intended to cause pain, yet it does not change the color of the heart, does not destroy nature. In other words, it does not kill but keeps alive.

148

"For the just shall live by faith" — by faith in the Savior. ✛ But this heart is fixed on the center of a white rose, to show that faith causes joy, comfort, and peace. The rose is white, not red, because white is the ideal color of all angels and blessed spirits. ✛ This rose, moreover, is fixed in a sky-colored background, to show that such joy of faith in the spirit is but a promise and beginning of heavenly joy to come. This joy, though not yet revealed, is looked forward to and held by the hope which we have. ✛ Around this background is a ring, to show that such bliss in heaven is endless. And since the ring is made of gold, the best and most precious metal, it also shows that the bliss of heaven is more precious than all other joys and treasures.

A Hero of Faith

Yes, Luther's power was the power of the Gospel. For learned and courageous though he was, without this Gospel — who knows? Would his name have reached down into our time?

We need not spend much time wondering. We know that he owned the Gospel's treasure and power, imperfect though he was. And perhaps we would do well to remind ourselves that Luther was imperfect. He had many faults. Yet even these served their purpose in God's plan for his life. As Melanchthon put it: "Some have complained that Luther was too severe. I will not deny this. But I will answer in the language of Erasmus: 'Because the sickness was so great, God gave this age a rough doctor.'" And again: "If Luther was severe, it was because of his earnestness for the truth, not because he loved strife or harshness."

This, then, is the story of Martin Luther, the Christian who fought his foes with the two-edged sword of the Scriptures. His birth was unnoticed by the world, yet his death brought grief to thousands. To this very day he lives on — a hero of faith inspiring new generations of boys and girls, men and women, to "grow up in every way into Him who is the Head, into Christ." (Ephesians 4:15)

149

A Martin Luther Calendar

. . . showing, at a glance, the important events of his life,
all but a few months of which he spent in Germany.

1483 — born November 10 in Eisleben, the second child of Hans and Margaret;
baptized November 11, the festival of St. Martin of Tours.

1484 — moves to Mansfeld at the age of six months.

1489 — enrolls in the Mansfeld Latin school at age four and a half.

1497 — begins a year at the high school taught by the Brothers of the Common Life in Magdeburg.

1498 — studies at the Latin school in Eisenach, where Dr. Trutvetter sees "something in that boy," and where Mrs. Cotta likes his singing.

1501 — travels to Erfurt to begin his university studies.

1505 — still at the University of Erfurt, studying to become a lawyer, when suddenly he enters the Augustinian monastery to take a monk's vows.

1507 — becomes a priest, celebrating his first Mass in May.
— returns to the university, this time to study theology.

1508 — goes to Wittenberg, to serve as a temporary teacher in Elector Fredericks' struggling university.

1509 — returns to Erfurt, where he becomes both a university teacher and a student.

1510 — packs for a trip to Holy Rome, a trip that makes him wonder.

1511 — back once more to Wittenberg, this time for good; teacher, preacher, and in —

1512 — *Doctor* Martin Luther, thanks to the University of Wittenberg faculty.

1514 — sees a bright light in his tower room, the light of Romans 1:16, 17, "The righteous shall live by faith."

1515 — made supervisor of eleven Augustinian monasteries, thus becoming a traveling man.

150

1517 — when Tetzel and Pope Leo's indulgences get too close to Wittenberg, he hammers down his *Ninety-five Theses* on October 31 — a Halloween never to be forgotten.

1518 — meets with Cardinal Cajetan in Augsburg, ready to be shown from the Scriptures where he has been wrong, only to be disappointed.

1519 — talks with Miltitz in Altenburg, hails the newly elected Emperor Charles V, and debates with John Eck in Leipzig.

1520 — keeps the printers busy with *An Address to the Christian Nobility of the German Nation, On the Babylonian Captivity of the Church,* and *The Freedom of the Christian Man;* becomes, according to Pope Leo, a wild boar who has invaded the Lord's vineyard, but burns the bull in a Wittenberg bonfire.

1521 — though excommunicated, dares to stand before the emperor at Worms, refusing to recant; kidnaped and put into the Wartburg for safekeeping, even before the emperor can issue the Edict of Worms; here, as Knight George, makes the New Testament speak German.

1522 — returns to troubled Wittenberg and works successfully to restore order.

1525 — denounces the peasant rebels, whom the princes defeat in bloody battles; decides he does, after all, have time for a wife, especially one Katherine von Bora.

1528 — joins others in visiting the Saxon churches, one reason why in —

1529 — publishes his Large and his Small Catechism; meets with Ulrich Zwingli and others at the Marburg Castle, where he argues that *is* means *is;* becomes a Protestant, even though absent from the Diet of Speyer.

1530 — obeys the elector's order to stay behind at the Coburg Castle, but wishes he were at the Diet of Augsburg to help Melanchthon's Confession and its Apology along.

1534 — turns the pages of the first truly German Bible, his translation of both the Old and the New Testament; cradles newborn Margaret, the last of his six children.

1536 — signs the Wittenberg Concord, which helps draw German Lutherans and Zwinglians together.

1537 — reworks the Schmalkald Articles till he is willing to stand on them even to his death.

1539 — with Melanchthon writes a letter approving Philip of Hesse's plan to add a second wife to the royal household, a letter he soon comes to regret having signed.

1545 — refuses to take part in Pope Paul's Council of Trent, which holds its first session in December.

1546 — leaves Wittenberg and dies in Eisleben February 18; laid to rest in the Castle Church in Wittenberg February 22, where his coffin remains to this day.

EMS R.

WESER R.

ELBE R.

ODER R.

RHINE R.

BRANDENB

Magdeburg

SAXONY

Leipzig

THU

Erfurt

Marburg

RINGIA

o Cologne

Aachen

Mainz

Trier

Oppenheim

Worms

Heidelberg

o Nuernberg

Speyer

Ingolstadt

Strassburg

DANUBE

BAVARIA

Augsburg

Munich

INN R.

Zurich

Einsiedeln

Glarus

SWITZERLAND

Trent

The Reformation Lands

Holy Roman Empire under Charles V

Black Forest

Magdeburg
ELBE R.
WESER R.
Wittenberg
Mansfeld
SAALE R.
Eisleben
Torgau
Halle
Frankenhausen
Leipzig
Grimma
Naumburg
Borna
Eisenach
Erfurt
Weimar
Altenburg
Wartburg
Jena
Schmalkalden
Orlamuende
WERRA R.
Coburg
Zwickau
Leipzig
Louvain
AUSTRIA
FRANCE
Zurich
Milan
Florence
ITALY
Rome
SPAIN